101 QUESTIONS

ABOUT YOUR SKIN THAT GOT UNDER YOUR SKIN ... UNTIL NOW

101 QUESTIONS ABOUT YOUR SKIN

THAT GOT UNDER YOUR SKIN... UNTIL NOW

FAITH HICKMAN BRYNIE

. . . .

Twenty-First Century Books
BROOKFIELD, CONNECTICUT

Published by Twenty-First Century Books
A Division of The Millbrook Press
2 Old New Milford Road
Brookfield, CT 06804

Cover photograph courtesy of Photo Researchers (© John Bavosi/SPL)

Photographs courtesy of Custom Medical Stock Photo: pp. 9 (© 1993 Robert Becker, Ph. D.), 10 (© 1994 Richard Wehr), 15 (© 1996 SPL), 135 left (© 1991 Keith) right (© 1989 CMSP); © Physicians Reference Gallery of Medical Art: p. 13 Science Source/Photo Researchers: pp. 26 (© Biophoto Associates), 72 (© D. Phillips), 113 top (© Eamonn McNulty/SPL) middle (© James Stevenson/SPL) bottom (© Dr. P. Marazzi/SPL); © 1994 United Feature Syndicate, Inc.: p. 51; Reuters/ Corbis-Bettmann: p. 63; Reuters/Archive Photos: p. 65 (© Jeff Christensen); AP/Wide World Photos: p. 70; Visuals Unlimited: pp. 77 (© SIU), 81 (© Bill Beatty), 89 (© David M. Phillips), 109 (© Ken Greer); Xeroderma Pigmentosum Society: p. 94; Phototake: p. 98 (© Ken Sherman); National Oceanic and Atmospheric Administration: p. 103; Flash Productions / © Charles Gatewood: pp. 140, 143

Library of Congress Cataloging-in-Publication Data
Brynie, Faith Hickman, 1946–
101 questions about your skin that got under your skin . . . until now / Faith Hickman Brynie.
    p.   cm.
Includes bibliographical references and index.
Summary: Uses a question-and-answer format to present information about the physical make-up and functions of human skin, hair, nails, as well as facts about diseases, effects of the sun, and more.
ISBN 0-7613-1259-5 (lib. bdg.)
1. Skin—Miscellanea—Juvenile literature. [1. Skin—Miscellanea. 2. Questions and answers.] I. Title. II. Title: One hundred and one questions about your skin that got under your skin . . . until now.
QP88.5.B78   1999
612.7'9—dc21   98-50695   CIP   AC

CONTENTS

The author gratefully acknowledges the expert critical reviews prepared by dermatologist Dr. Barry Goldberg of Danbury, Connecticut, and by Dr. Bonnie Baxter, Biology Program Chair at Westminster College in Salt Lake City. Their willingness to contribute their time and expertise assured that this book was as accurate as they and the author knew how to make it.

Grateful appreciation also to Dan and Caren Mahar of the Xeroderma Pigmentosum Society and to Jennifer Lloyd and her family for all their sharing, caring, and advice. Thanks also to Martha Crockett Lancaster for her assistance with Charles Baudelaire and all matters French.

FOREWORD

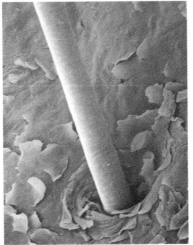

What is it? A power pole on a mountaintop? An arrow fallen to earth? No, it's a hair growing from human skin as seen by a scanning electron microscope. As otherworldly as this picture seems, it can scarcely begin to hint at the wonders of human skin.

If you're like most people, you probably never think much about your skin. You probably take for granted that it holds you together, makes you look like you, and always erupts in zits at the most embarrassing times. Is there more?

A great deal more, which you can begin to explore in this book with the answers to questions people often ask about that complicated organ, skin. Have you thought of skin as an organ, a coordinated system of tissues that carries out important life functions? It's true. Skin is an organ as complex and essential to survival as your heart, kidneys, or brain. Skin regulates temperature, prevents water loss, and fights infection.

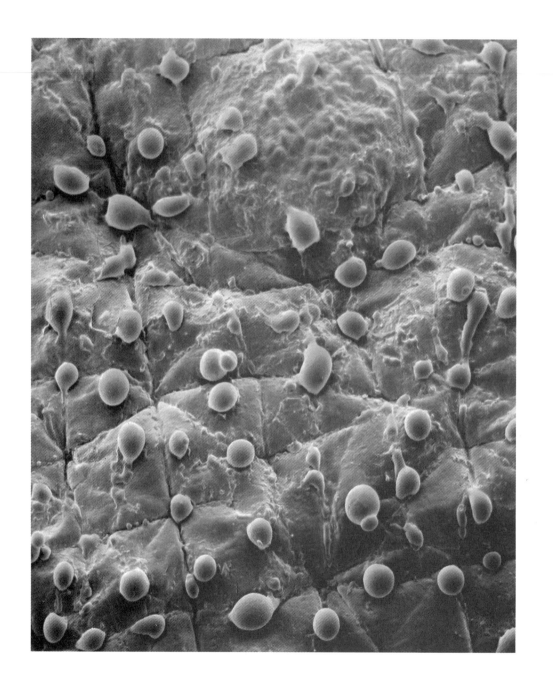

Skin also tells our brains much of what we know about our environment and situation. Touch a hot stove and you'll pull your hand away—a response that prevents serious injury. Indeed, touch may be the most finely tuned of all human senses. Have you ever been alone in a room, only to suddenly feel certain that someone had joined you, although you neither saw nor heard anyone? That feeling of "not-aloneness" happens when tiny hairs covering the body's surface trigger receptors in the skin. These nerve endings can inform the brain of changes in temperature and air currents so slight that you don't consciously notice them.

All this should convince you that there is more to skin than meets the eye. Did you know, for example, that hair and nails are modified forms of skin? Hair grows from deep "pockets" beneath the skin's surface. It's made of the same protein as the skin's outermost cell layer. Fingernails, too, are made of that same protein. The living cells that produce both hair and nails lie within the skin's lower layer, the dermis.

In this book, you'll learn what's on, in, and under your skin. You'll get answers to questions that "got under your skin...until now." Begin your exploration of skin's living landscape with the picture on page 10. Can you guess what it is? See "In Closing" on page 146 for the answer.

CHAPTER ONE

18 QUESTIONS THAT SHOULD COME FIRST

The skin, like a cloak, covers us all over, the oldest and the most sensitive of our organs, our first medium of communication, and our most efficient of protectors.

• ASHLEY MONTAGU •

What Is My Skin Anyway?

Let's face it. Unless you get a new pimple or break out in a rash, your skin is probably the last thing on your mind. Your skin—as Montagu points out—covers and protects, communicates and informs. But as long as it's working perfectly (as it most often does), you probably take it for granted.

You may not realize, either, how complicated your skin is. Look at the back of your hand. What appears to be nothing more than a thin covering—maybe something like a latex glove or a sheet of plastic wrap— is actually the heaviest, although not the largest, organ in your body. (The digestive tract has a greater total surface area than the skin.) What you see is merely the surface of the skin's top layer, the epidermis.

Like the rest of the body, skin is made of cells. (Cells are the basic structural units of nearly all living things). The epidermis is some 15 to 30 cells thick,[1] about as thick as a sheet or two of paper. The outer surface, often called the horny layer, is made of dry, dead, flattened cells that have lost their nucleus. (The nucleus is the command and control center of living cells.) The horny layer is aptly named because its cells contain a lot of the tough, hard material know as keratin.

Beneath the horny exterior lies a granular layer of squamous cells. Deeper still are the basal cells. They divide continuously, giving rise to new skin cells that gradually move toward the skin's surface. The cells of the horny layer fall off constantly, replaced by others pushed up from the basal cells below. The renewal takes about a month.[2]

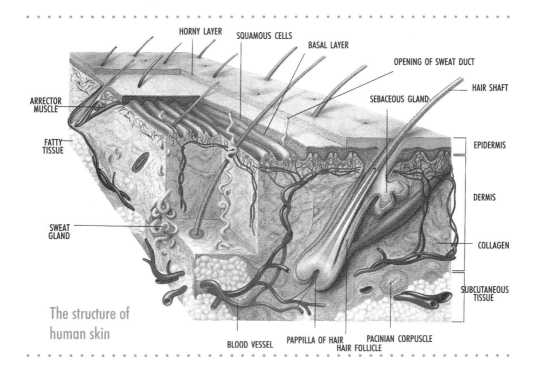

The structure of human skin

Melanocytes, or pigment cells, also make up part of the epidermis. Controlled by a hormone secreted by the pituitary gland in the brain, they produce melanin, which gives skin its color. One out of every six cells in the basal layer is a melanocyte.[3]

The epidermis has no blood supply. Scrape your skin and it will ooze clear liquid, but you'll see no blood. It's only when it penetrates into the layer below that an injury bleeds. This deeper layer is the dermis. It accounts for about 90 percent of the skin's volume and mass.[4]

The dermis contains blood vessels, oil glands, sweat glands, nerve endings, and hair follicles. Although embedded in the dermis, a hair follicle is actually an in-pocket of the epidermis. (Imagine poking a finger into rising bread dough. You'd make a tunnel to the interior of the bread, but the walls of the tunnel would still be the exterior surface of the bread.)

Sebaceous glands opening into follicles make an oil that lubricates skin and hair. That oil, called sebum, makes skin soft and smooth and protects it from infections. The flow of sebum sweeps dead cells and bacteria out of the follicle. Sebum also keeps hair pliant and gives it its shine.

In the dermis, cells called fibroblasts make collagen and elastin. Collagen makes skin strong and attaches the epidermis to the underlying tissues. (If you want to see collagen, simply look at a piece of leather. It's collagen from the cow's dermis.) Elastin lets it stretch and spring back like a rubber band. Collagen provides strength, and elastin delivers flexibility.

Below the dermis lies the subcutaneous layer of collagen strands, connective tissue, and stored fat. Here too are the arteries and veins that carry blood to and from the tiny capillaries that feed the dermis. The fat deposited in the subcutaneous tissue has several important functions. It provides a reserve of energy for emergencies when food is scarce. It also absorbs shocks and protects the body from extremes of heat and cold.

To a chemist, your skin is about 70 percent water, 25 percent protein, and 5 percent other materials including fats and minerals.[5] The most important components in skin, as in other parts of the body, are the proteins. Proteins are the major molecules making up muscle, internal organs, the brain—even that 20 percent of blood that is not water.[6]

Proteins are chains of smaller units called amino acids. These building blocks are made of carbon, hydrogen, oxygen, and nitrogen atoms. Three of the 20 amino acids that make up human protein also contain sulfur.

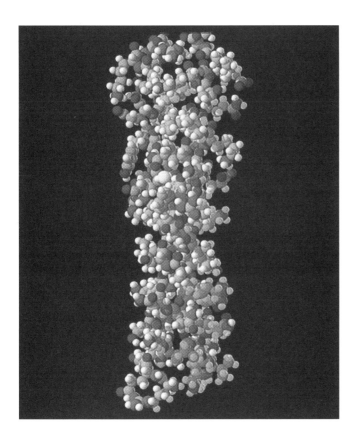

A ball-and-stick model of a keratin molecule. The amino acids, joined like beads on string, twist into a helical (spiral staircase) structure. Helices then wrap together to form a super helix, as shown.

Proteins may be one, two, or more chains of amino acids bound together. The chains twist into the three-dimensional shape of a complete protein. The amino acids they contain and the shapes they form give proteins different properties. That means the proteins in skin differ from the proteins of muscle, blood, or brain both in how they are built and in what they do.

All cells contain two categories of proteins: structural proteins that make up the cell itself, and enzymes. Enzymes accelerate chemical reactions, including the manufacture of other proteins. Cells in the different layers of skin differ in their protein composition. For example, about 80 percent of the cells in the epidermis make the hard material keratin, which is—you guessed it—a protein.[7]

About a third of all body protein is collagen.[8] It's the major fibrous part of skin. It also composes most of the cartilage at the joints, the tendons that attach muscles to bone, the ligaments that hold bones together, and even the bones themselves.

What Does My Skin Do?

Skin is much more than a bag that holds your bones, muscles, and internal organs together. For one thing, it plays a big part in regulating the body's fluid balance. Skin is very nearly waterproof. It lets no water in even if you soak in the tub for hours on end. Perhaps more important, it lets hardly any water out—only a liter or less per day.[9] Water loss through the skin helps hold body temperature steady, regardless of the weather or your level of activity.

The elastin and collagen of the dermis act as both support structures and shock absorbers. Their fibrous network is filled with a protein gel called ground substance, which makes skin sturdy yet pliable. The subcutaneous layer of fat insulates the body and protects muscles, bones, and internal organs. Hit your hand against a table, and the skin bounces back. Turn a cartwheel and your skin bends and twists with the movements of your joints and muscles. Gain or lose weight and your skin expands or contracts with your changing size. It's nature's own "shrink to fit" material.

Your skin is also the body's first line of defense against poisons and diseases. If undamaged, the horny layer forms an almost impenetrable barrier to disease-causing microbes.

For those invaders that do manage to get through, the epidermis has another weapon waiting—the Langerhans cells. Somewhere between two and four of every hundred epidermal cells are of this type.[10] These cells have an ability essential to fighting disease: they can distinguish "self" from "not self." When Langerhans cells detect an invading protein, they trigger a series of steps that lead to the capture of the invader by cells of the immune system and its transport to the fluid-filled vessels of the lymphatic system.

Skin cells also work as tiny chemical factories. They produce vitamin D when exposed to sunlight. They make interferon and interleukin, two among many proteins important to the body's immune defenses. They also manufacture several important hormones, proteins that regulate the action of other organs in the body. Skin even acts as a storage depot for water, sugar, calcium, and other important nutrients and minerals.

Is My Skin a Sense Organ, Like My Nose or My Ear?

The skin is the sense organ that lets you detect pressure, pain, heat, and cold. Receptors in the skin send messages to the brain that let you tell a kitten's fur from a bristle brush—even with your eyes closed. Your skin can alert you to danger, too, be it a spill of boiling water or the bite of a mosquito.

On a patch of your hand about the size of a postage stamp, some 134 yards (123 meters) of nerves terminate in about 9,000 nerve endings.[11] Receptors on these nerve endings are specialized in the stimulus they respond to (and therefore the message they send to the brain). Some detect pain; others respond to pressure, light touch, continuous touch, and cold or heat. Receptors are inside layers of jellylike material. When receptors for touch or pressure are squeezed together, the layers inside slide across each other and initiate a nerve impulse.

Receptors are either "on" or "off." They either send a signal or they don't. So how can your brain tell warm from hot or a slight sting from a deep cut? The intensity of the signal is a result of the number of receptors firing at any one time. The greater the number of receptors stimulated, the stronger the sensation.

For example, your skin can tell a light breeze from a strong wind because nerve endings in hair follicles respond to movements that affect the hair. If only a few move, the day is balmy; but if many move, it's time to run for cover. Your skin doesn't need much time to alert you to action, either. When stimulated, these nerves send their signals to the brain in less than one-hundredth (0.01) of a second.[12]

Some areas of skin are more sensitive than others. The tip of your tongue and the ends of your fingers are especially sensitive because they contain many receptors packed closely together. The back of your hand is less sensitive than the palm because receptors there are fewer in number and farther apart.

Sensory receptors in the skin perform one other bit of magic you may not have thought about. They detect the amount of force you apply when making a movement such as forming a fist or gripping an object. The truth is, you don't know your own strength. Without the sensory information your skin sends to your brain, you could rip a muscle from a bone doing nothing more complicated than picking up your dinner plate. Your skin lets you know just how much force is the right amount to get the job done without injuring yourself.

Your skin is also an important organ of communication. You can say "I love you," but your facial expression can carry the opposite message because of the complex arrangement of muscles and skin in the face. The wide eyes of fear or the spread lips of joy communicate across all languages, all cultures. The touch of a hand can reveal love or hate without words.

Touch is so important that some claim it's the one sense essential to survival. A human being can live without sight, hearing, smell, or taste, but deprived of touch, an infant will fail to thrive, perhaps even die. In the late 1980s a series of experiments showed that premature babies who were touched and massaged gained weight more rapidly than "preemies" considered too sick and delicate to touch. Massaged babies were more alert, slept better, and scored better on mental and motor tests. On the average, they left the hospital six days earlier than the infants given standard intensive care.

A loving touch for anyone—child or adult—boosts circulation and releases chemicals into the blood that relieve pain and lessen anxiety. Massage has been shown to boost the immune system of AIDS patients. Some corporations give free massages to their employees to increase productivity by relieving headaches, back strain, and fatigue. Workers who enjoy twice-weekly massages are more alert and work faster, studies show.

What Causes an Itch?

Think of an itch as a pain that isn't hurting yet. If some irritant stimulates the pain receptors in the skin lightly, the brain interprets the signal as a tickle. Stimulate a little more, and the tickle becomes an itch. The stimulation comes from the release of the protein histamine in the skin. (The over-the-counter cures are appropriately called antihistamines). Lots of different things can cause that release, including chemicals, temperature changes, friction, insect bites, dry skin, germs, stress, and anxiety. Any number of diseases can induce itching including hepatitis, gallstones, kidney failure, thyroid disease, and some liver ailments.

Itching makes you want to scratch, but scratching provides only short-term relief. No one is quite sure why. Some scientists think scratching masks pain signals with pressure cues. Others believe it may temporarily inactivate pain receptors.

How Does My Skin Help Cool Me on a Hot Day?

Your skin acts a lot like a thermostat. Heat sensors in the skin act as switches. When you're too warm, the body allows greater heat loss. When you're cold, heat conservation measures kick in.

For example, when you exercise strenuously, the day is warm, or you are ill with a fever, an increased load of heat moves from the body tissues into the blood. The hypothalamus (a gland in the brain) detects the change and sends messages to the skin, signaling capillaries in the dermis to expand and surface blood flow to increase. This allows heat to pass from deep within the body to the skin's surface where it can be lost to the air. The loss of heat is achieved through the physical processes of convection, conduction, and radiation.

Sweating helps cool the body, too, but not directly. The cooling effect is the result of the evaporation of moisture from the skin's surface. It takes a lot of energy to change perspiration from liquid to gaseous form. Heat from the body provides this energy. Play squash vigorously for an hour and you lose more than a quart (from 1 to 1.5 liters) of water through sweat. In hot weather, you can lose up to 3 gallons (more than 10 liters) of water a day through sweat glands.[13]

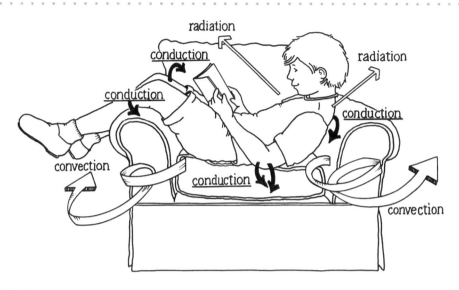

The skin loses heat by conduction, convection, and radiation. Sit on a cold chair and you'll warm it by conduction, which requires contact. Convection is the loss of heat to air currents. Even in a still room, air currents pass over the skin, taking heat with them. Radiation means simply that rays of heat emanate from the body and spread in all directions.

In the cold, sensors in the skin prompt different actions. Heat conservation measures take over. Surface blood vessels contract. Sweat glands go dry. You shiver and tiny hairs on your arms stand on end, trapping a layer of warm air close to your skin.

How Much Skin Do I Have?

Laid flat, the skin of an average adult male would cover the top of a twin-size bed (about 20 square feet or a little less than 2 square meters).[14] Depending on your size, your skin weighs about as much as a healthy newborn baby—somewhere in the range of 6 to 10 pounds (2.7 to 4.5 kilograms).[15] Add the underlying layer of subcutaneous fat, and your outer covering weighs about 20 pounds (9 kilograms).[16]

Why Do Some People Have Oily Skin and Some People Have Dry Skin?

It all depends on the sebaceous glands. These glands, which open into each hair follicle, make an oil called sebum. Sebum rises to the surface from the hair follicle and mixes with perspiration. The resultant oil-water emulsion makes skin feel oily.

Many people have a greater density of sebaceous glands on the nose, chin, and forehead, which makes those areas feel oilier than the cheeks or neck. Also, some people's sebaceous glands are more active than those of others. The more sebum the glands produce, the oilier the skin feels.

When the weather is humid, sweat evaporates from the skin more slowly, so skin may feel especially oily on a hot day. While this may feel uncomfortable, it is usually less of a problem than excessively dry skin.

What Makes Skin Different Colors?

Skin color comes mostly from the pigment called melanin. (Careful: Don't confuse melanin with melatonin, a protein available in drug and health-food stores that some people claim promotes sleep.) People with pale skins turn brown in the sun as their skin makes more melanin. Freckles and moles are darker because they contain more melanin. There are two kinds of melanin: eumelanin (black and brown) and pheomelanin (red).

Carotenes, the same compounds that make some vegetables yellow or orange, give skin a yellowish tinge. Everyone's skin contains some carotene, but large amounts make Asian skin look more yellow than other skins. Hemoglobin is the red, oxygen-carrying pigment in blood. In skin containing little melanin, it may show through giving very pale skins a pinkish cast.

No matter what your skin color, you have the same number of melanocytes (the pigment-producing cells in skin) as everyone else—about 60,000 per square inch (about 6.5 square centimeters).[17] The more than 30 different colors of skin recognized by experts result from a variety of factors, including:

- the amount of melanin each melanocyte produces;
- how fast the pigment is made;
- how the pigment is arranged in the skin cells;
- the depth at which the granules lie (deep melanin granules give skin a blue or gray sheen.)
- the type of melanin.[18]

In dark-skinned people, the melanocytes are more active than in light-skinned people. They produce more melanin. People of African ancestry have large granules of melanin within their skin cells, and the cells are completely filled with pigment. In fair-skinned people, the granules are fewer and smaller. Two advantages of dark skin color are a lower incidence of skin cancer and fewer wrinkles. However, dark skin is more likely to change color when injured than is pale skin.

The brain controls the activity of melanocytes. The pituitary gland signals another gland, the hypothalamus, to produce a protein called melanocyte stimulating hormone (MSH). The more MSH sent out from the brain, the more melanin produced. Melanin gives the body a natural protection against sunlight.

The loss of skin color is called vitiligo. It affects about one in every hundred people and frequently begins when you're young.[19] No one knows for sure what causes the skin to suddenly begin losing its color, usually in well-defined patches. It may happen because the body's immune system attacks melanin-producing cells, mistaking them for foreign invaders such as viruses. Another idea is that some abnormal chemical produced by the nervous system blocks the production of melanin. People with vitiligo are usually healthy, and the loss of pigment poses no health risk, although it may cause worry and loss of self-esteem. Skin stains and makeup can improve appearance, and medical treatments can sometimes help repigment the skin.

Changes in skin color can sometimes alert doctors to disease. Very pale skin may reveal anemia (lack of iron or hemoglobin in the blood). When starved for oxygen, skin turns blue. A classic sign of carbon monoxide poisoning is a bright, cherry-red color, while poor liver function can cause the skin to turn yellow (called jaundice).

Is All Skin the Same Thickness?

On the average, the outermost layer of skin is about the same thickness as one or two sheets of paper.[20] The epidermis varies in thickness from less than 1 millimeter to more than 4 millimeters.[21] It is thickest on the parts of the body that contact the environment most—the palms of your hands and the bottoms of your feet, where it's about 3 to 6 millimeters (0.1 to 0.2 of an inch) thick. The thinnest skin is on the eyelids. It's about half a millimeter (2/100 of an inch) thick.[22]

How Much Dead Skin Do I Shed in a Day?

Try a quick test. Stick a piece of clear tape to the back of your hand. Pull it away. Hold it up to the light. What you see, along with some dirt and oil, are hundreds of dead skin cells. If they weren't on the tape, they would end up on the furniture, your bed, your towel, or the shower floor.

You lose about 10 billion dead skin cells every day. That's the weight of a penny every three days,[23] or about 50 pounds (nearly 23 kilograms) in a lifetime.[24] See that dust on your bedside table? As much as 75 percent of that dust is dead cells from your skin.[25] But don't worry too much. Young people get new outer coat cells every three or four weeks,[26] although skin renewal for those in their thirties or forties can take twice as long.[27] Believe it or not, people shed their skins more often than snakes.

Is It True That Tiny Creatures That Feed on Skin Cells Live in My Mattress?

In your mattress and on you, too. In *Gulliver's Travels*, Jonathan Swift imagined a race of miniature people he called the Lilliputians. In the poem "Conversation," he wrote about tiny living things of the very real variety:

So, naturalists observe, a flea
Hath smaller fleas that on him prey;
And those have smaller still to bite 'em;
And so proceed ad infinitum.

Swift captured a truth there. Every living thing is an environment—a home to other living things. Millions, even billions, of bacteria live on your skin harmlessly and peacefully most of the time. You can't wash them off, nor should you. These "friendly" bacteria live in the horny layer of the epidermis where they feed on dead cells and body wastes. They earn their keep by producing chemicals much like antibiotics that prevent disease-causing organisms from invading the skin and causing infection.

A dust mite

Mites that live in your mattress, pillows, carpets, and furniture are a more serious matter, since many people are allergic to them. Many different kinds of eight-legged mites feed on skin cells, mold, pollen, fibers, plant material, soil particles, animal dander, and many other "foods" available in ordinary house dust. They are about 0.3 millimeter long—smaller than the period at the end of this sentence—and virtually invisible to the naked eye. They have no eyes and no breathing structures. They thrive in warm, moist, food-rich environments like your bed. An old mattress can easily contain more than a pound (about 450 grams) of dust composed mostly of skin cells.[28]

The best cure for allergies to dust mites is prevention. Vacuum bedding and furniture often. Wash sheets and blankets often; air pillows and cushions. Replace old mattresses, sofas, and carpets if the problem is severe.

What Is Sweat?

Sweating is involuntary. You can't make it happen, and you can't stop it from happening. Even when the weather is cold and you're sedentary, you lose somewhere between a half-liter and a liter (a quart or less) of water through the skin daily.[29] This perspiration, which you don't notice, is not produced by sweat glands. It's simply diffusion of water molecules from the epidermis into the air.

When your body temperature rises, tiny muscles around the sweat glands contract, squeezing perspiration out through the pores. Hot weather, alcohol, certain foods and drugs, exercise, fever, and emotional stress shift sweat glands into action. What's the body losing when you sweat? Sweat is about 99 percent water.[30] Dissolved in it are salts of sodium, potassium, and magnesium. Sweat also contains tiny amounts of waste materials such as urea (the major toxin in urine).

Your skin contains some 3 to 5 million sweat glands,[31] the combined total of two different types. Most abundant are the eccrine glands, about 2 million of them distributed over the entire body.[32] These glands empty directly onto the skin through pores. They help control body temperature and excrete waste material. They're at work when sweat rolls down your chest on a hot day.

The eccrine glands handle the body's heat-regulating functions. Exercise increases both the size and the efficiency of eccrine sweat glands. If you work out regularly, after a few weeks you'll start sweating at a lower body temperature and come to tolerate heat better.

The second kind, the apocrine glands, are inactive in childhood. They begin to work between the ages of 10 and 14 when the production of sex hormones increases. They empty into hair follicles mostly in the armpits and groin. They produce a thick, colored fluid containing a complex mixture of fats, water, and proteins. The apocrine glands are especially sensitive to emotions. Antiperspirants work only on the apocrine glands.

Perspiration itself is odorless, whether it comes from apocrine or eccrine glands. It's only when bacteria grow in sweaty places, such as under the arms, that odor occurs. In many animals, such odors are an important means of communication. If humans communicate with scents, we are unaware of it, and we are likely to mask our natural smells with artificial deodorants, soaps, and perfumes.

About one in every 100 people sweats to excess—a medical condition called hyperhidrosis. Most common among people of Asian ancestry, the disorder can be both uncomfortable and embarrassing, especially in social situations where shaking hands may mean extending a palm dripping with sweat. Surgeons can now help with an operation that removes the nerves that stimulate sweating of the palms. Several nonsurgical methods are also available for treatment.

Although sweat rids the body of some wastes, don't believe the claim that you can sweat away poisons from the environment, infections, or food allergies. Sweating can't cure anything. In truth, because perspiration robs the body of water, vigorous exercise can make you feel worse if you're suffering from a cold or the flu.

Sweat, however, can reveal drug use. The chemical remains of alcohol, amphetamines, cocaine, heroin, methadone, morphine, and phencyclidine (PCP) all show up in human sweat within an hour or two of drug use. They will continue to be excreted for several days—even weeks—which is why sweat patches are sometimes used for drug testing.

Any stimulus that arouses the "fight or flight" response subjects your body to stress. Meet up with a large, growling dog, for example, and your body immediately switches into high gear. Your heart beats faster. The blood supply to your brain and muscles increases. Your liver pumps a hefty dose of glucose (the sugar the body uses as fuel) into the bloodstream. Your pupils dilate and you breathe faster. You also sweat more, especially from the apocrine glands.

The body also has a separate system of sweat glands—notably in the palms of the hands—that secretes when you're under stress. Have you ever heard that an animal can sense your fear? No one knows whether that's true, but it's possible that the animal can smell the profuse secretions of your sweat glands.

Remember a time when you faced a threatening dog, and you may find that you experience fear just as you did during the real event. Imagining the incident can produce the same result. The stress need not be physical. Think about a big test in school, public speaking, or a blind date, and you may feel the "fight or flight" sensation.

Yes and no.

Take in too few calories (too little energy) or deprive the body of protein foods, and skin problems can result. Severe malnutrition, starvation, food allergies, or deficiencies of vitamins or minerals can all show themselves as skin disorders.

But these are the extremes. Assuming you eat a healthy variety of foods, no single food or food supplement is going to change your skin—either for better or for worse. No matter what the commercials claim, there's no magic formula for clear skin, shining hair, or strong nails.

Your body manufactures the proteins according to the "instructions" contained in the nucleus of your cells. Assuming your diet provides all the raw materials your body needs, there's nothing you can do to alter that natural process.

Does My Skin Absorb Water From the Air?

No, it's just the opposite. Skin loses water to the air.

That's where the cosmetic industry comes in. Moisturizers are nothing more than fats or oils that sit on the skin's surface and slow the rate of water loss. Glycerin (an ingredient in some moisturizers) may bind water that would otherwise evaporate from the skin's surface, but it can't return it to the dermis. But, then, it doesn't really need to. If a moisturizer slows the rate of water loss, skin will feel softer and look smoother. Preparations containing alpha hydroxy acids (AHA) and Retin-A can make skin look less wrinkled, but not by causing water absorption. They work by peeling away outer, dead skin cells revealing smoother, firmer cells beneath.

Why Do My Fingers Get Wrinkly When I Soak in the Bathtub?

Leave a grape in the sun and it will dry out, becoming a wrinkled raisin. It makes sense that plump, round fingers might pucker in the tub for the same reason; but, in truth, just the opposite occurs.

The skin is covered with a protective layer of sebum. When soap and water remove that oil and some of the dead skin cells at the surface, water can soak into the dead cells of the horny layer. Saturated with water, these cells expand and pile up on one another. Your fingers and toes, where the skin is thickest, end up looking like raisins.

After an hour or two, the water evaporates from the horny layer and the skin smoothes out again.

Can Drugs Penetrate the Skin?

Some can. Most cannot unless the skin is cut or damaged.

Normal, healthy skin is an effective barrier against virtually all large molecules. Forget advertised claims that wrinkles vanish when vitamins or collagen are applied to the skin. These molecules are simply too big to work their way past the horny layer.

There are, however, exceptions to this rule. The skin of newborn babies is highly permeable (easy to penetrate). Drugs or chemicals that contact an infant's skin can pass easily through the epidermis and into the blood. Even in adults, penetration is possible, often with serious consequences. Poisoning and even death resulting from contact with herbicides, pesticides, and industrial chemicals are not uncommon.

On the positive side, drug-impregnated patches can take advantage of the skin's permeability to deliver beneficial medicines to the bloodstream. Patches are painless, nonirritating, and can discharge a steady, measured dose. Drugs that can be taken this way include scopolamine for motion sickness, nitroglycerin for heart disease, and nicotine for breaking the cigarette habit. Soon, women may be able to use estrogen patches for hormone replacement after menopause.

Before long, too, the needle-less injection—as on "Star Trek"—may become a reality. Robert Langer at the Massachusetts Institute of Technology built a device he called a sonicator. Its low-frequency sound waves cause air bubbles in the fatty parts of the skin's horny layer to expand and burst. That weakens the solid fat, changing it to a liquid. Relatively large molecules such as insulin can pass through the liquid oil into the muscle and blood beneath. After about an hour, skin permeability returns to normal.

Synesthesia

When touched in specific ways, I see colors. I always have. Often, the colors are seen bright and luminous: azures, greens, and blues against a black background as dark and rich as silk velvet.

CAROL STEEN

Have you ever listened to Ferde Grofé's *Grand Canyon Suite*? Hearing that music seems to transport the listener to the Canyon. The melodies and rhythms evoke mental images of majestic cliffs, rocky trails, and plodding donkeys hauling heavy packs from the Canyon's rim to the muddy Colorado River far below. When Grofé spins up a lightning storm, the listener can almost feel the rain.

Almost. For most of us, Grofé's music is simply bringing back memories. We have experienced—either in real-life or on TV—the clip-clop of donkeys and the roar of thunder. It is easy for us to relate these sounds to visual memories.

But for a small number of people, listening to music is an entirely different experience. Some people see sound as color. Others experience touch and sight in combination. Artist Carol Steen writes:

> *The colors (I see) differ depending on what touches me. The bright piercing orange of the dentist's drill dissolves the black background and hurts my eyes. The acupuncturist's needles cause colors along my legs, my arms: greens, reds, pinks and yellows. I can tell what points are connected to the other linked points by the colors.*[33]

People like Carol are called synesthetes, a term that means "those who combine the senses." The phenomenon is called *synesthesia*.

The nineteenth-century French poet Charles Baudelaire describes synesthetic experiences in his poem "Correspondances," meaning associations. To Baudelaire, echoes mix together as shadows. Some smells are the sound of an oboe; others are the green of meadow grass. Experts aren't sure whether Baudelaire was a genuine synesthete or if he was simply writing metaphorically.

Most of us use many synesthetic metaphors in everyday communication, scarcely thinking about what we're saying. When friend Ida proclaims she's "all points and plugs today," her meaning is clear: She's feeling out of sorts, edgy, nervous.

But true synesthesia is much more than figurative language. The combining of senses is real for those who experience it. In his book *The Man Who Tasted Shapes*, Richard Cytowic tells of his friend Michael, who wouldn't serve a chicken dish until it had enough points on it. To Michael every flavor had shape, temperature, and texture. He felt and sometimes saw geometric shapes when he tasted or smelled food. Some flavors produced a touch sensation throughout his whole body. Others he felt only in his hands. Michael literally grasped the shape, fingered the texture, and felt the weight and temperature of flavors and smells. For example, Michael sensed mint as "cool, glass columns":

I can reach my hand out and rub it along the back side of a curve. I can't feel where the top and bottom end: so it's like a column. It's cool to the touch, as if it were made of stone or glass. What is so wonderful about it, though, is its absolute smoothness. Perfectly smooth. I can't feel any pits or indentations in the surface, so it must not be made of granite or stone. Therefore, it must be glass.[34]

Synesthetes typically experience their "joined" senses for many years before learning that others do not perceive the world as they do. Writes Alison Motluk:

Like most synaesthetes, I grew up assuming that everyone saw numbers and letters and words in colour, as I did. In my late teens, I abruptly learned that this was not the case. I was discussing a short story with my high school English teacher, trying to explain to her why the main character's name should not be changed. It had to be a 'strong, red name,' I remember saying, appealing to reason. She was intrigued, and asked me to elaborate, but warned me that 'other people don't think that way.[35]

How many of us experience some of our senses in combination? Richard Cytowic estimates that one in every 100,000 individuals "is born to a world where one sensation involuntarily conjures up others," but he suspects that figure is too low. Hearing words, letters, or numbers as colors is the most common form of synesthesia. British scientists suspect that as many as one in every 2,000 people can do it.[36] Professor Joel Norman of the University of Haifa thinks that perhaps one person in ten has some synesthetic ability without knowing it.[37]

No one knows how synesthesia works, but we can guess that some kind of cross-communication between the brain's sensory pathways must be involved. Evidence also suggests that synesthetes:

- inherit their cross-sensory abilities from their parents.
- are more often women than men.
- are often left-handed or ambidextrous.
- have normal nervous systems and mental health.
- are often highly intelligent and have excellent memories.
- sometimes experience certain learning or thinking difficulties, such as a poor sense of direction or trouble with math.

One thing is certain: Synesthetes have no control over their perceptions. They can no more stop themselves hearing colors or tasting shapes than the rest of us can block out the music of an orchestra or the taste of chocolate. "Mine is a universe of black '1s' and pink 'Wednesdays', numbers that climb skyward and a roller-coaster shaped year," writes Alison Motluk. "The astonishing realization for synaesthetes is not that these characters are imbued with colours but rather that a world could exist in which they were colour-free, neutral, characterless."[38]

CHAPTER TWO

19 QUESTIONS ABOUT HAIR

Babies haven't any hair;
Old men's heads are just as bare;
Between the cradle and the grave
Lies a haircut and a shave.

• SAMUEL HOFFENSTEIN •

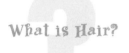

What is Hair?

Pluck a single strand of hair from your head and you have lost what scientists call the hair shaft. The shaft is made of three layers, each inside the other. The outer casing is the cuticle. Under an electron microscope the cuticle reveals itself as a series of overlapping layers, something like shingles on a roof.

Inside the cuticle lies the cortex, a column of cells containing keratin, the same protein that hardens tooth enamel and fingernails. The central core of the hair is the medula. Also called the pith, it is made of small, hardened cells snared in a web of fine filaments.

What you left behind when you pulled out that hair was the follicle, a tiny pouch below the scalp's surface that manufactures hair. The hair follicle obtains a rich supply of nutrients from the tiny blood vessels that surround it. Sebaceous glands that open into the hair follicle produce the oily sebum that lubricates hair and skin. Arrector muscles around the follicle can—quite literally—make your hair stand on end.

At the bottom of the follicle is the papilla, an upward-growing finger of connective tissue. The papilla forms the root of the hair. The part of the hair that is actively growing is the hair bulb. The cells that generate the hair lie just above the hair bulb. As soon as hair cells are manufactured, they harden and die, forming the hair shaft.

The thick, colored hair that grows on your head is called terminal hair. Somewhere between 65 and 95 percent (by weight) of terminal

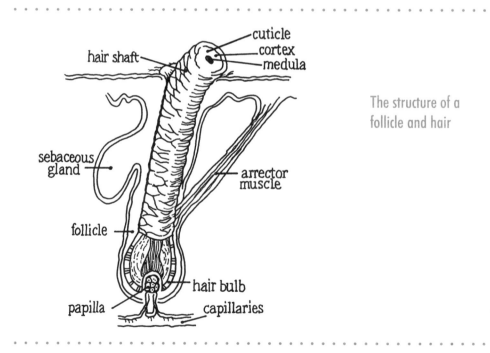

The structure of a follicle and hair

hair is protein.[1] Other components of hair include water, fats (lipids), pigment (color), and trace elements (minerals). Because proteins twist into complex three-dimensional shapes held together by chemical bonds, hair is both rigid and flexible. The strength of hair comes mostly from its middle layer, the cortex.

Is All Hair Alike?

No. The downy hair that grows on a fetus is called lanugo hair. Soon after birth, it is replaced by vellus hair. Vellus hair covers the skin's entire surface except the palms of the hands and the soles of the feet. It is fine, nearly colorless, and slow-growing. It lasts a lifetime and is scarcely visible except with a magnifying glass.

Some people have silky, fine terminal hair, while others sport strong, coarse hair. These differences arise from variations in the diameter and shape of the hair follicles. The positions of bonds between sulfur atoms account for curls, too. A perm works by rearranging such chemical bonds.

The smaller the diameter, the finer the hair. Curly hair has more "body" than straight hair for two reasons. First, curly hairs are thicker than straight hairs. Second, they bend into one another, making the hair stand out from the head more.

African, Asian, and Caucasian Hair Look Different. Are They Really?

The basic structure is the same for all human beings, but characteristics vary. Slice a straight hair from an Asian person crosswise and you may see (under a microscope) that the hair shaft is round. People of African ancestry usually have curly hair that is flattened in cross-section. Caucasian hair is more nearly elliptical. Both Cau-

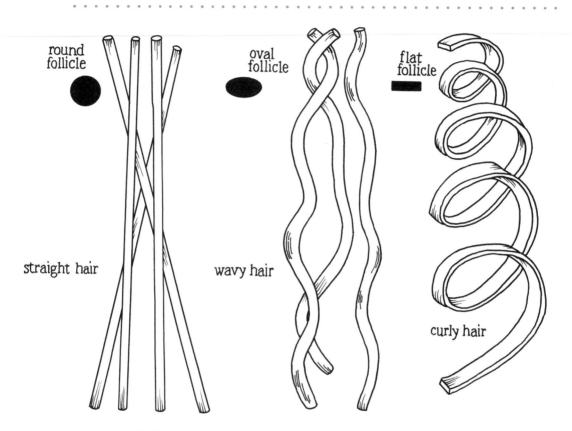

round
follicle

oval
follicle

flat
follicle

straight hair

wavy hair

curly hair

The diameter and shape of the hair follicle makes hair curly or straight.

casian and African hair is usually smaller in diameter than Asian hair. Coarse hair from a beard often looks triangular or kidney-shaped.

The shape and texture of your hair are inherited from your parents in complicated ways. The kinky hair of African peoples is often dominant (showing up in the offspring) over the straight or wavy hair of Caucasians. Among Europeans, curly or wavy hair is usually dominant over straight hair, but the straight hair of American Indians seems to be dominant over the curly hair of Europeans.

Ethnic groups differ also in when they turn gray. On average, Caucasians notice their first gray hairs at age 34; those of African ancestry, at age 44. Asians are intermediate, starting the graying process in their late 30s.[2]

Does Hair Serve Any Real Purpose?

Today we use our hair more as a statement of who we are than anything else. When you cut, style, straighten, perm, or color your hair, you are (perhaps unconsciously) communicating something about your identity, your character, and your membership in a group. For modern people, hair is a social statement.

But hair has not lost its biological functions. Although humans are hairless or nearly so, we actually have more hair follicles per unit of skin area than monkeys, chimps, and gorillas.[3] We only seem hairless because vellus hair is so short and fine. But even that downy coat helps keep you warm and protects against extremes of heat and cold. Hair also helps combat water loss. Body hair has a sensory role to play as well. The movement of hair on the skin helps you detect even the lightest touch or change in temperature.

The hair on your head cushions your head against blows and protects your scalp from sunburn. When the weather is cold, hair slows loss of heat from the head. A layer of hair provides insulation, and the high sulfur content of keratin gives it heat-retaining properties.

Eyelashes keep dirt, insects, and foreign objects out of the eyes. Eyebrows keep sweat from running down from the forehead into the eyes. The hair inside your ears, coated with the waxy substance cerumen, traps dirt, insects, and infections that might damage the delicate tissues of the inner ear. Hair in your nose filters dust and germs from the air.

You were born with all the hair follicles you'll ever have. You lose quite a few as you grow older, and some change what they do, but you never produce any new ones. Furthermore, the follicles get farther apart as you grow. On average, a newborn baby has about 1,135 hair follicles per square centimeter of scalp area. By the time the baby is an adult, the number is nearly half at 615.[4] An adult male has about 5 million hair follicles on his entire body.[5]

The average scalp contains between 80,000 and 120,000 hair follicles.[6] You probably have the higher number if you're a blond, the lower number if you're a redhead. Brunettes usually fall in the middle, with about 100,000. The number of hairs may be deceptive however. Red hair is usually thicker and coarser than blond hair so it appears fuller. Hair is thickest between the ages of 15 and 30.[7]

Measured in diameter, the finest hairs vary from 0.017 to 0.050 millimeters, the coarsest from 0.064 to 0.181 millimeters.[8] Women's hair is usually slightly thicker than men's. A child's hair is usually finer than an adult's.

By the way, you probably have somewhere between 90 and 200 lash hairs on each upper eyelid. The lower eyelid has only 60 to 100, and they're shorter.[9]

No. Hair growth and replacement occur in three stages. The anagen phase is when hair actually grows. At any time, some 80 to 90 percent of the hairs on your head are in this phase.[10] Growing hair remains on the scalp for about three years,[11] although the growth period can be as short as two years or as long as six[12] in different people. (The hair of the eyebrows and eyelashes is the exception to the rule. Eyelash hairs last about three months before they fall out.[13] Eyebrows grow for about ten weeks, then rest for nine months.[14] That's why it takes so long for eyebrows to grow back after they are shaved.

At any time, about 3 or 4 percent of the hairs on your head are in the catagen phase.[15] The hair stops growing for a week or two. The hair follicle slows its production of protein and pigment, and the lower segment of the follicle breaks down. As the growing part of the hair disappears, the upper part of the hair forms a club hair. It separates from the papilla and falls out. Some people mistake the white tip of a club hair for the hair's root and believe that the hair will not be replaced. They're wrong. It will. Club hairs are normal shedding and not a reason to worry. It's normal to lose between 50 and 100 hairs each day.[16]

The resting phase, called telogen, lasts several weeks or months.[17] About 13 percent of normal scalp hairs are in the telogen phase at any time. Then, the anagen phase begins again, and hair growth resumes.

How Fast Does Hair Grow?

If you are one of those people who can grow hair to your waist, you have a long anagen phase. If you can't grow hair past your shoulders, your anagen phase is short. But even hair that seems to grow slowly is being produced at a phenomenal rate. Considering how many hairs you have, over an average long weekend, you'll grow more than a football field's length of hair.[18] That's more than a mile of hair per month, or about 7 miles (11 kilometers) per year![19]

Not all hair grows at the same rate. Hair on the top of the head grows fastest, averaging 0.44 millimeter each day. Males grow hair on their chins almost as quickly at 0.38 mm per day. Eyebrow hair is the slowest growing of all—a mere 0.16 mm per day.[20] Eyebrow hair stays short because the growth phase lasts for only ten weeks. Eyelashes are replaced every three months. You'll grow about 600 eyelashes in your lifetime.[21]

Although their hair is less dense, females on average grow hair a little faster than males. In women, more hair tends to remain in the anagen phase during pregnancy, making hair seem particularly thick and lustrous at that time. The normal cycle returns later, however, and women often notice what seems like excessive hair loss after their baby is born. This increased shedding can last from one to six months,[22] when the normal growth cycle resumes.

How Can I Make My Hair Grow Fuller, Thicker, Faster?

You can't. Some people think hair grows faster or thicker after it is shaved. Science has proven otherwise. Hair from any individual follicle grows at a constant rate. Some people think hair grows faster at night. Not so. Hair production is steady 24 hours a day. The menstrual cycle doesn't affect the rate of hair growth. Nor is it true that shampooing hurts your hair or that massaging the scalp will prevent hair loss.

As long as you consume a normal diet, no food or food supplement can change the quantity or quality of your hair. Furthermore, there's no way to "feed" hair from the outside. Hair is made of dead cells that won't absorb vitamin E, protein, or any nutrient no matter how convincing the advertising. Certain products that coat the hair shaft make it thicker, but only until your next shampoo. Perms and colors plump up the hair shaft, but hair grows back according to the genetic code contained in the nucleus of body cells.

Why Does My Hair Get Frizzy When It Rains?

The wetter the weather, the greater the number of water molecules floating in the air. Dampness in the air is measured as humidity. In the

80 to 90 percent humidity of a swamp, you'll feel moist and uncomfortable. In the 20 percent humidity of a desert, you'll feel much drier. When it rains, the humidity in the air rises. Water molecules work their way into spaces in the hair's scaly cuticle. They push the scales apart, increasing the volume of the hair shaft. The result? A bad hair day!

Why Do Men Grow Hair on Their Faces and Women Don't?

Facial hair grows in males only after puberty. At that time, production of male hormones increases. One male hormone, testosterone, is produced by the testicles. It stimulates the growth of both facial and body hair in men.

Women may produce increased facial and body hair, too, as a result of male hormones produced normally by the adrenal glands. Usually, the amount is small and women notice little, if any, facial and body hair. In some ethnic groups—for example, those of Mediterranean ancestry—greater amounts of body hair are normal in women. Rarely, excessive hair growth in women signals a disease of the adrenal glands or ovaries, and medical attention is required.

Why Do Some Older Women Grow Hair on Their Faces?

It's not really new hair but a change from the peach-fuzz (vellus) hairs into longer, coarser, darker hair. The reason is menopause. As production of the female hormone estrogen decreases, the relative concentration of male hormones normally produced by the adrenal glands rises. That means that the male hormone is not present in any greater quantity, but constitutes a greater fraction of the total of all hormones circulating in the blood. The increased "load" of male hormone can cause the hair on the head to become thin and wiry, and dark hairs to appear on the upper lip, chin, and cheeks.

Put a single hair under a microscope, and you'll see granules of black, brown, yellow, or red pigment. What you see are tiny particles of melanin, the same pigment that gives skin its color. In the papilla of the follicle, melanocytes produce melanin, which is deposited in the cortex of the hair shaft. As the hair grows upward, pigment continues to form in the cells of the cortex. Some hair follicles make more pigment than others. Usually the hair of eyebrows is the darkest-colored hair on the body.

As with skin, there are two kinds of melanin. Eumelanin makes hair black or brown. Pheomelanin makes it red or blond. Only redheads—or those carrying the genes for red hair—make pheomelanin. Auburn hair results from pheomelanin nearly hidden by eumelanin, and pheomelanin present in small amounts can make black hair shiny.

Pigment production can vary with age. Often Caucasians who are blond in infancy produce darker hair as they grow older. The gray or white hair of old age results from a loss of activity in the melanocytes. In young people, an enzyme called tyrosinase breaks apart the amino acid tyrosine as an important step in the manufacture of melanin. As people get older, less of that enzyme is produced, so less melanin is made. Eventually, the hair shaft grows out with little, if any, pigment in the cortex. What's left is the color of the keratin itself—a yellowish gray.

Dyes and bleaches change more than the color and texture of hair. They change it chemically as well. Temporary colors simply coat the hair shaft and wash away easily. Permanent dyes penetrate the cuticle and alter the structure of the hair shaft. Hydrogen peroxide bleaches dark hair by destroying melanin granules. Lighteners, dyes, and waving solutions produce a marked reduction in the amount of cysteine (a sulfur-containing amino acid) in hair.

Do Hair Dyes Cause Cancer?

That's a controversial question lacking a clear-cut answer. In 1985 scientists in Baltimore reported an association between exposure to hair dye and leukemia, cancer of the blood cells. Three years later, the *American Journal of Public Health* suggested that cosmetologists, beauticians, and hairdressers developed certain cancers more often than did people in other occupations. They asserted, furthermore, that people who dye their hair are also at greater risk.

In 1992 a large-scale study by the National Cancer Institute agreed. Dyes, they said, might contain cancer-causing substances that could be absorbed through the scalp. The darker the color and the longer the dye is used, the greater the risk, the Institute charged.

But by 1994 new information challenged those assertions. Researchers at Brigham and Women's Hospital in Boston studied the medical records of 99,000 nurses between 1976 and 1990. They found no higher incidence of cancer in those who dyed their hair than in those who never had. An American Cancer Society study that same year garnered similar findings. Men who dyed their hair faced no greater cancer risk. For women, the situation was mixed. Hair dye increased by 50 percent a woman's chance of a form of cancer called non-Hodgkin's lymphoma. But that risk is still small. The disease strikes only 11 of every 100,000 women in the United States.[23]

By 1994 yet another National Cancer Institute study concluded that the link between hair dye and cancer was "incredibly weak." It showed—surprisingly—that those who had colored their hair at some time in their lives actually had a decreased risk of some fatal forms of cancer. Using black hair dye for more than twenty years was the only undisputed danger, and it was small. Opposing views have kept the controversy going: "Women should not be afraid they will get cancer from coloring their hair," concluded the press.[24]

"Women may wish to consider how important it is to dye their hair," said a spokesperson for the National Cancer Institute.[25]

In 1997 researchers at Michigan State University reported a higher incidence of cancer of the salivary glands (the glands in the mouth that secrete saliva) among hairdressers as compared with women in other occupations. Dyes may not be the culprit in this case, though. The cause may be airborne chemicals inhaled from permanent waving solutions or hair sprays.

Has Anyone Ever Really Turned Gray Overnight?

According to legends, Sir Thomas More in the sixteenth century and Queen Marie-Antoinette in the eighteenth went gray overnight when informed of their impending executions. Many have believed in such occurrences, including poets such as Lord Byron, who writes, in *The Prisoner of Chillon* (1816):

> My hair is gray, but not with years
> Nor grew it white
> In a single night,
> As men's have grown from sudden fears.

Though history has alleged it and poets have proclaimed it, overnight graying is impossible. Hair is dead, and fright, trauma, or stress— no matter how many stories you hear to the contrary— cannot remove the color it contains. Normal graying happens gradually, as less melanin is laid down in the hair shaft over time.

Graying can happen in relatively young people. Diminished activity of the adrenal or thyroid glands and pernicious anemia (a deficiency of vitamin B_{12}) can cause hair to gray early. Genetics plays a part, too. Some people inherit the tendency to gray while still young. Stress, illness, or trauma may also speed up graying.

So does any kernel of truth lie behind the legends? Maybe. Sometimes, the body's immune system goes haywire and attacks its own proteins. One such autoimmune disorder results in rapid hair loss, because immune cells attack the follicles. If pigmented hair is lost rapidly while unpigmented hair remains behind, the hair may appear to gray rapidly. Perhaps that's what happened to those doomed characters the historians and poets wrote about.

What Is Dandruff?

Just as you continuously lose cells from the epidermis of your skin, so too is the skin of the scalp constantly shedding, taking about 28 days to complete the cycle. But when scalp cells migrate to the surface and mature in only five or six days,[26] you may notice a dusting (or a drift!) of large white flakes along the shoulders of your favorite navy blue sweater. Nearly everyone has some, but about one in every four of us finds it excessive or itchy.[27] Doctors call it seborrhea, but most of us know it as dandruff—annoying, embarrassing, unattractive dandruff.

No one knows what causes the sloughing of cells to speed up, but it's not dry skin, soap, or hair spray as some people think. It might be a mild inflammation of the scalp or the action of some microorganisms such as bacteria or fungi. It might be some hormone, a dietary excess or deficiency, irritation from a cosmetic or chemical, or excess production from the oil glands. Dandruff runs in families, so maybe there is a hereditary component. Even stress or trauma might trigger the production of dandruff.

The good news is that dandruff isn't contagious. It doesn't lead to serious skin problems, and it won't cause your hair to fall out. Over-the-counter dandruff shampoos control flaking by minimizing the accumulation of scalp skin. Check the label of your favorite dandruff shampoo and look for one or more of the following ingredients:

- pyrithione or ketoconazole, antimicrobial agents thought to kill a kind of yeast suspected as a cause of dandruff;
- salicylic acid or sulfur, which loosens scales so they are washed away more easily;
- menthol or other anti-itch formulations;
- cortisone preparations that relieve itch, slow flaking, and reduce redness and swelling;
- coal-tar extracts that decrease flaking;
- selenium sulfide, which slows the rate of cell maturation and reduces scaling.

More serious than dandruff is seborrheic dermatitis in which large, greasy yellowish scales with crusts appear behind the ears, in the groin, or on the chest or face. The hair becomes excessively greasy. The scalp becomes itchy and inflamed. This condition requires a doctor's care.

What Causes Hair Loss?

Are you one of those people who worry that their hair will fall out if they worry that their hair will fall out? Although worrying about hair loss can't cause hair loss, stressful situations can. Physical illness, hospitalization or surgery, injury, or the death of a loved one may all provoke hair loss in some people. Some forms of mental illness can cause hair loss, as can eating disorders such as anorexia nervosa. (Curiously, severe anorexia also causes the growth of a fine, downy fur all over the body.)

Alopecia areata is the medical term for the loss of hair in patches, usually on the scalp, beard, eyebrows, or pubic area. Alopecia may result from fever, surgery, allergies, crash diets, burns, scalds, and tumors.

Other possible causes include radiation exposure, glandular disorders, diseases of the liver and kidneys, and a variety of illnesses from flu to scarlet fever. A deficiency of iron, zinc, or certain vitamins is at the heart of some cases, as is chemotherapy for cancer. Hair loss is a side effect of many drugs, including some blood anticlotting agents, gout and arthritis medicines, certain antidepressants, beta blockers (used to control irregular heartbeat and high blood pressure), large doses of certain vitamins, birth-control pills, and hormone replacement treatments for menopause. Some studies have associated stressful life events with the onset of alopecia.

Alopecia areata affects about one in every hundred people at some time in life.[28] That's about 2.5 million men and women in the United States alone.[29] It is seldom serious or permanent, but it can be disturbing—even frightening. A doctor can prescribe various treatments, but it usually gets better on its own within six months to a year.[30]

Losing Some Hair Is One Thing. Going Bald Is Another. What Causes Baldness?

About 21 million women and 35 million men in the U.S. experience significant hair loss.[31] Women usually notice a general thinning of the hair all over the scalp or a balding spot at the crown. Men typically experience loss at the hairline and crown first. Later, hair disappears from the top of the head, leaving a band of normal hair growth around the sides and back. This male pattern baldness affects 40 percent of men ages 18 to 39 and 94 percent of men over the age of 80.[32]

Baldness doesn't happen because hair growth suddenly stops. Neither the number nor the structure of hair follicles changes. Instead, they gradually shrink and become less active, producing shorter, finer hairs.

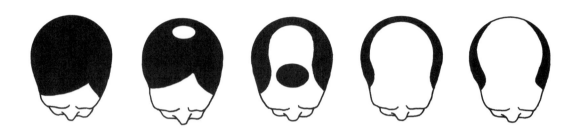

The usual progression of male pattern baldness. As first, the front hairline begins to recede, followed by balding at the crown of the head. Baldness continues gradually until a "horseshoe" of hair is left.

The tendency toward baldness is inherited. Genetic programming controls the age when hair loss begins and how fast it progresses. In 1998 researchers at Columbia University discovered a human gene associated with human hair loss. (A gene is a piece of DNA in the nucleus of a cell. Genes determine what proteins a cell makes and, therefore, what characteristics the cell will have.) They named the gene "hairless" and suggested that it may be the gene that turns on the human hair growth cycle.

Heredity alone, however, is not enough. Three interacting factors—heredity, hormones, and aging—cause the change in follicles. Male hormones (even in women) must be present for balding to occur. And the process usually does not begin until a person's twenties or thirties, although some men begin to lose hair in their teens.

No matter what you read in the ads, poor circulation, inadequate blood supply, emotional problems, clogging of the hair follicles, bad diet, and blood "poisons" do not cause baldness. Nor it is true that bald men have higher levels of male hormone than men with full heads of hair. Instead, the hair loss seems to have something to do with increased sensitivity of hair follicle cells to the normal levels of male hormones. Some evidence suggests also that an enzyme (called 5 alpha reductase) is more active in men who lose their hair than in those who do not. This enzyme converts the male hormone testosterone into a different form.

As in males, female hair loss results from a combination of factors: hormones, heredity, and aging. Fewer women than men suffer from hereditary hair loss, and the loss is usually less extensive. As estrogen levels decline at menopause, hair loss increases, but female hair loss is not confined to middle age. The number of young women losing their hair may be rising. Hugh Ruston of the University of Portsmouth in England believes that increasingly more women are losing their hair because of the stresses of their careers. Simultaneously coping with demanding work environments and caring for families may increase a woman's sensitivity to the small amounts of male hormone that circulate in her blood. The result? Hair loss in females who carry the genes that promote hair loss in men.

Among both women and men, no serious physical effects arise from hair loss except the need to protect the head from sunburn and heat loss. The real threat from baldness is psychological. Although baldness doesn't seem to have hurt the careers of actors Patrick Stewart, Ted Danson, Bruce Willis, or Sean Connery, some bald men lose their confidence and self-esteem along with their hair. Women are vulnerable too. A survey in England found that three out of four women who experience hair loss feel less attractive, and one in three feels that losing her hair is the most disturbing event in her life.[33]

Is a magic hair-growing potion possible?

Do Hair-Growing Lotions Work?

Maybe Dilbert's creator has found a magical, hair-growing spray, but no one else has. No spray, lotion, or pill can reverse baldness in its later stages. Some progress has been made, however, in slowing the rate of hair loss earlier, while the hair is growing. Minoxidil (tradename Rogaine®) was used as a treatment for high blood pressure. Then doctors noticed a curious side effect. The drug caused hair to grow. When applied to the scalp, it either slowed the rate of hair loss or promoted the regrowth of hair in about 25 percent of men and 20 percent of women.[34] The Food and Drug Administration approved it as a prescription-only treatment for baldness in 1988. In 1996 it became available over-the-counter in this country. Another drug, finasteride (tradename Propecia®), was approved in 1997 as a prescription drug for hair loss in men.

What Is a Hair Transplant?

More than 40,000 Americans take advantage of surgical alternatives every year.[35] One such surgical procedure is the transplant or graft. To graft hair, the surgeon removes small cylindrical pieces of scalp from the sides and back of the head and transfers them to the top. Sometimes openings to receive the grafts are made with a steel punch; sometimes a carbon-dioxide laser is used. Under local anesthetic, some 20 to 50 "plugs," each containing from 4 to 15 individual hairs, may be moved in about an hour.[36] The procedure may need to be repeated several times to effect any noticeable improvement.

Scalp reduction is also performed under local anesthetic. The surgeon cuts away a portion of the hairless scalp. The remaining scalp is then stitched together, reducing the total area of baldness. Scalp reduction may be performed once or even twice before hair transplantation.

Still another surgical alternative is flap surgery. In this procedure, a thick flap of hair-bearing scalp is sliced only partially so it is still attached, then turned to cover the spot where a flap of bald scalp has been removed. The flap site heals with a scar that can be covered by surrounding hair.

The Hair Analysis Controversy

. . . .

Cowlicks are lucky. Two crowns predict death by drowning or living on two continents. Combing hair after dark causes forgetfulness. Eating bread crusts or eggs makes hair curly. Men with hairy arms are strong or rich. Bald men are virile and smart.

SUPERSTITION, FOLKLORE, AND OLD WIVES' TALES

. . . .

Since the snake-haired Medusa of Greek myth turned to stone those unfortunate enough to gaze on her, Western culture has suffered no shortage of fantasy and fiction about hair. Dark-haired women are faithful and trustworthy. Redheads have hair-trigger tempers. Blondes are unreliable. A hair that falls over the nose foretells wealth. Counting the teeth in a comb brings bad luck.

Few people today seriously believe that hiding clippings of hair under a rock prevents baldness, but how many of us have been fooled by so-called "scientific" claims about hair analysis? Some promises for the "miracles" of hair analysis are daydreams at best and frauds at worst. Other uses of hair analysis are both valid and useful.

For example, hair analysis has settled some historical debates. Beethoven's hair cleared him of the charge of taking morphine for his kidney stones. The poet John Keats's opium habit showed up in his hair. Napoleon did not die of arsenic poisoning, his hair revealed. Archaeologists have even uncovered the diets and diseases of past civilizations from tiny samples of hair.

Hair analysis is important to forensic science. Forensic science is the process of gathering and examining evidence that can be used in a court of law. The Federal Bureau of Investigation has used it for years. Sometimes just the shape, texture, and color of hair when seen through a microscope is enough to place a suspect at the crime scene. In other cases, forensic scientists can extract DNA from hair samples if a few of the living cells of the hair's bulb have been shed at the crime scene. DNA is the hereditary material in the nucleus of cells. It's unique for each of us (except identical twins). If the DNA in blood, semen, saliva, or hair matches a suspect's DNA, a conviction is likely.

Educators think that hair analysis might someday help kids with behavioral problems and learning disabilities. One concern is lead. Dutch researchers found that children with high concentrations of lead in their hair had slower reaction times than other children. High lead levels also predicted poor performance on some other learning tasks. Robert Tuthill at the University of Massachusetts reported that children who had trouble paying attention were also likely to have high levels of lead in their hair. Researchers at Appalachian State University demonstrated that lower lead levels meant improved behavior in school.

By far the most accepted use of hair analysis is for the detection of drug use and abuse. Because it's cheaper, urine samples are tested more frequently than hair. But that picture is changing fast, because urine testing has drawbacks. Drugs such as cocaine, methamphetamine, and opiates are processed quickly in the body. They may not show up in urine after three days. Hair analysis, on the other hand, can uncover the use of marijuana, amphetamines, opiates, cocaine, and PCP as far back as three months.

How does hair testing detect drug use? The bloodstream supplies hair-forming cells in the follicle with food and oxygen. Drugs circulate in the blood, as do certain products—called metabolites—that the body manufactures from the drugs. Drugs and their metabolites get locked into the hair's core. Since hair grows a little more than a centimeter each month, hair analysis can disclose not only which drug was taken, but also when. Hair tests can also determine whether drug use is increasing or decreasing.

Hair testing is not perfect, however:

- The rate of hair growth varies among individuals; differences in growth rate can affect the estimate of when a drug was ingested.
- Hair testing costs as much as three times more than urine testing.
- To determine whether drugs have been used recently—say, within the past week—hair must be plucked, not cut, which can be painful.
- Hair analysis results can vary with different procedures and among different laboratories.
- People who don't smoke marijuana but have been around those who do can test positive.
- False positive tests for illegal drugs can result from the use of legal, over-the-counter medicines, including some painkillers, diet pills, and cough syrups.
- Experts aren't sure whether hair testing is accurate for all racial groups.
- Experts also disagree about the amount of a drug in the hair that actually proves drug use.

The biggest objections to drug testing are not scientific but legal, ethical, and moral. Is it right for an employer to invade an employee's privacy with drug testing? Is it fair to deny jobs to those who have used drugs in the past but may be "clean" now? What about the use of drug-testing results? Can they legally or rightfully be turned over to police or judicial authorities?

In general, the courts have upheld the rights of employers to test for drugs. The Supreme Court of Nevada ruled that hair testing is a reliable means for detecting drug use. It also held that a positive test for cocaine use was sufficient reason to deny unemployment benefits. But the laws are complicated. For example, the Americans with Disabilities Act protects people who were addicted in the past but does not cover current users of illegal drugs. Lawyers can argue long and hard over the definitions of past and present use.

While hair analysis for drug use is generally reliable, its use for judging health and nutritional status is not. Ads in newspaper and magazines have touted hair analysis as a magical path to better health and well-being. Hair analysis and nutritional supplements have been sold to a gullible public as magic cures for poor memory, fatigue, overweight, stress, heart disease, and much more. With costs ranging from tens to hundreds of dollars, self-proclaimed hair analysts provide "test results" along with sales pitches for vitamins, minerals, or herbs costing tens and hundreds of dollars more.

Analysis for nutritional deficiencies has several drawbacks. For example, although people with certain skin diseases have been found on average to have lower levels of magnesium in their hair than those with healthy skin, the two groups overlap so much that a test for magnesium in the hair offers no value for diagnosis. Also, there's no evidence that taking magnesium pills helps cure those skin diseases. Hair testing is also unreliable for other minerals such as zinc, for which shampooing and dyeing can affect tested levels.

Dr. Stephen Barrett sent identical samples of hair to 18 commercial laboratories. The reports differed widely. Reported values failed to match up. So did the definitions of normal levels. A mineral rated low in one report was judged normal or high in others.[37] Although hair analysis has some legitimate uses in research, it "isn't at a place where it's of general use to consumers," says Dr. Donald Hensrud of the Mayo Clinic.[38]

In 1985 the Federal Trade Commission (FTC) took action against a bogus hair analysis scheme. The following year, authorities in New York shut down a lab and a health-food store for using hair analysis findings to recommend vitamin and mineral supplements. As a result, hair analysis schemes pop up less frequently now than they once did, but they still tempt consumers. "Hair analysts are just taking advantage of people," Hensrud says.[39] Barrett calls commercial hair analysis "quackery...unscientific, economically wasteful, and probably illegal."[40] Elmer Cranton, author of *Trace Minerals, Hair Analysis, and Nutrition* agrees: "Sending hair for analysis through direct mail—well, a lot of that is just marketing hype and abuse."[41]

CHAPTER THREE

QUESTIONS ABOUT NAILS

Her fingers make me see petals,
The lotus' are like that.

• *LOVE POEMS OF ANCIENT EGYPT, AUTHOR UNKNOWN* •

Are Nails Important for Anything Except Looks?

Nails protect the sensitive ends of fingers and toes from injuries and chemicals. They help us to grasp and pluck small objects. Nails aid in our sense of touch. Although nails are dead and have no nerves, the nail bed beneath is remarkably sensitive to the impact signals that come in when you type, play the piano, or simply drum your nails in boredom. Nails can be tools for construction or weapons for defense. And they're just the thing when an itch has to be scratched.

Have you ever noticed that the doctor looks at your nails when you get a routine physical? The reason is that nails provide an early warning of some diseases. "Clubbing of the nails," in which the fingertips swell, can be a clue to lung disease. Opaque, white nails can signal cirrhosis of the liver. White bands on the fingernails may indicate arsenic poisoning. On the operating table, the anesthesiologist may check for a bluish purple color that warns that the sedated patient needs more oxygen.

What Are Nails Made Of?

Nails are actually an extension of the skin. They are made of keratin, that same hard protein that toughens the outer layer of the human epidermis and forms hooves, talons, feathers, horns, scales, and claws in other animals. Keratin is so tough that Henry Ford extracted it from soybeans and used it to make steering wheels in the cars of the 1930s. But compared with many other materials, the protein is quite soft. On the Moh scale of hardness that geologists use for rocks, soft talc gets a score of 1 and the hardest stone, diamond, rates a 10. A steel file gets a 7; glass, a 5.5. A fingernail earns a lowly 2.5, a little softer than a copper coin.

How Are Hair and Nails Alike?

Both hair and nails are made of keratin, but that's not all they have in common. Both grow from a specialized growth center deep in the dermis: the follicle (in the case of hair) or the matrix (in the case of the nail). The growth site is the only part of the hair or nail that's alive. The part that's visible is dead.

Because nails and hair are dead and have no nerves, you can cut them without pain. Both will continue to grow if cut or broken, but there's nothing you can do to make either grow any faster, stronger, or prettier. Nails are made mostly of protein and water. Calcium plays a minor role. Taking gelatin or calcium tablets will do no more to harden nails than eating carrots will curl hair.

Nails have two parts: what you see and what you don't. The keratin plate of the nail (the part you see) is produced by a zone of the epidermis called the matrix (the part you don't see). The matrix lies beneath the skin and behind the nail. You get a glimpse of the matrix through the lunula, the pale, half-moon at the base of the nail that extends back into the skin of your finger.

The thin, nearly transparent flap of skin surrounding the sides and base of the nail is the cuticle. It seals the matrix to the nail plate and keeps dirt and germs from invading the living tissue beneath it, the nail bed. Blood vessels are plentiful in the nail bed, making nails look pink except at the ends where they lose contact with the skin below and appear white.

The structure of a fingernail

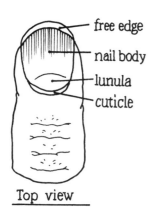

Top view

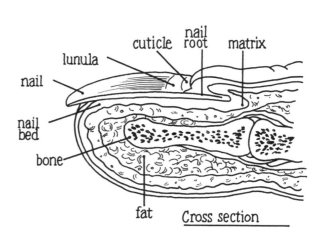

Cross section

How Fast Do Nails Grow?

Nails grow all the time—on average of about 1/8 inch (3 millimeters) per month.[1] Fingernails grow three times faster than toenails. A fingernail takes about 3 to 5 months to grow out; a toenail, as long as 15.[2] Nails grow faster when the weather is hot and when healing after injury. The nails of the middle fingers grow faster than the rest. The little fingernail grows the slowest, and the nails on the hand you use most grow faster than those on your less favored hand. Starvation diets slow the growth of nails.

Children's nails grow faster than those of adults. In a person's twenties, nails thicken and their growth slows. Before age 40, vertical or horizontal ridges appear. With increasing age, nails become drier and more brittle and may turn yellow from a buildup of keratin.

Do Nails Really Continue to Grow After Death?

No. Drying and shrinking of the soft tissues of the fingers may make the nails of a corpse appear to have grown. Hair doesn't grow after death either, although the scalp may shrink making hair look longer.

What Causes Those Little White Spots on My Nails?

The moon-shaped lunula is made of cells that are still laying down the protein keratin. If anything interferes with the hardening process, white spots or streaks may result. Most people have such spots occasionally or often. Sometimes spots result from injury or infection. Other causes include nutritional deficiencies, thyroid conditions, and anemia. Overzealous filing, manicuring, and nail biting can also be the culprits.

Why Do My Nails Crack, Layer, and Split?

Most likely, the answer is genetic. The cells of your matrix lay down a chemically and structurally weak nail plate compared with that of the lucky few persons who effortlessly grow iron-hard nails 2 inches (5 centimeters) long. So there's not much you can do to change the basic makeup of your nails, but you can be wary of environmental factors that make matters worse. Nails that are often in water and cleaning solutions may dry and split. Nail polish protects nails against water loss, but polish removers dry nails out, so frequent polishing and repolishing are not a good idea. Too much filing or improper cutting can separate keratin layers, causing flaking and thinning.

What Is a Hangnail?

A hangnail is a strip of dead skin that splits away from the area beside the fingernail. The term also describes a bit of torn cuticle at the base of the nail. Although minor, hangnails can be painful because of the rich supply of nerve endings in the tips of the fingers. Too much time washing dishes, bathing, or swimming can bring on a hangnail, as can nail biting or careless manicures. The best treatment for a hangnail is to cut it with scissors (don't pick or pull!) and cover with a Band-Aid until it heals. If a hangnail becomes infected, see a doctor.

What Is an Ingrown Toenail?

Computer screens flickered and printers hummed on October 16, 1997, as PR Newswire reported the hottest sports scoop. Michael Jordan had been forced to cut short his walking tour of Paris because of an ingrown toenail.

The legendary Michael Jordan goes up for a jump shot.

While some reporters chuckled over the story, coaches and fans of the Chicago Bulls weren't laughing. Ingrown nails severe enough to hinder walking can wreak havoc with dribbling and jump shots. Luckily for his team, Michael was soon back on the court, running up a score the sportscasters could laud.

Jordan knows from experience how an ingrown toenail looks and feels. When the hard plate of a toenail grows into the surrounding skin, the tissue becomes inflamed and infected. It swells, reddens, and hurts.

The tendency toward ingrown nails runs in families, but other things can cause them. Fungus infections, tight shoes, and improper cutting of the toenail can induce ingrowth. So can irritation from repeated activities in sports (such as kicking a ball) or injury to the nail (for example, dropping something heavy on it). Once you've had an ingrown toenail, your likelihood of getting another increases.

To reduce the risk of an ingrown toenail, wear shoes that fit (stay away from narrow toes and high heels). Don't cut toenails in a curve but straight across, past the end of the toe.

Is Nail Biting a Seriously Bad Habit? How Can I Break It?

If you bite your nails, you're not alone. Nearly a third of Americans ages 4 to 30 do it, too.[3] So do actors Emma Thompson and Arnold Schwarzenegger, TV journalist Maria Shriver, talk-show host Ricki Lake, world champion motorcyclist Michael Doohan, and cover girl Julie Delpy.

It's a habit worth breaking, not so much because it damages the nails but because of what it can do to teeth. Nail biters often suffer swollen and infected gums. A piece of fingernail that works its way into the gum can result in inflammation or even the loss of a tooth. Nail biting causes excessive wear and fractures of the teeth. It also transfers germs from hand to mouth so nail biters face an increased risk of colds, flu, and other infections.

One of many possible approaches to breaking the habit may work for you. Wearing gloves or tying strings around the fingers sometimes prevents nail biting long enough to break the habit. Some of those foul-tasting chemicals painted on the nails may help, too. An alternative activity, such as chewing gum, may take your mind off nail biting. Focusing your attention on the habit—becoming aware of it and telling yourself "Stop!"—may help as well.

If all that fails, try positive thinking. In his book *Learned Optimism*,[4] psychologist Martin Seligman recommends conquering bad habits by banishing critical self-talk. Don't tell yourself you're a failure because you bite your nails. Remind yourself that you are a winner who can achieve any goal you set for yourself.

Whatever your approach, don't expect it to be easy. Have you heard the story about Danny Wuerffel, the quarterback of the Florida Gators? When badgered by reporters for biting his nails, he proudly proclaimed a few months later that he had kicked the habit. His glory was brief. In 1996, the same year he led his team to its first NCAA championship and won the Heisman Trophy, *Sports Illustrated* reported that "his old demon came back to haunt him. He was chewing his fingernails again."[5]

Winner of the 1996 Heisman Trophy, Danny Wuerffel

You are looking at fungi (the singular is fungus) when you find mildew on the shower wall or mold on stale bread. These organisms are a little like plants, but far more primitive. We live in peace with most fungi, and some actually help us by performing neat tricks like making cheese. Some, however, can infect human tissue. Those that infect nails thrive on a diet of keratin, the protein that makes up the nail plate.

Fungal infections of toenails and fingernails are usually more unsightly than painful, but they do require medical attention since they can cause the loss of the nail. When infected with fungus, the nail becomes thick and brittle, turning an opaque white, gray, brown, or yellowish color. It doesn't itch or hurt unless the skin around the base becomes infected. Fungus infections of the fingernails usually happen after some injury, but infections of the toenails seem to happen for no reason at all. Hot, humid conditions—either of the weather or inside shoes and socks—increase their risk.

For reasons not well understood, fungal infections of the nails are three to four times more numerous now in the United States than they were 20 years ago.[6] Some sources say that 10 to 12 million Americans are infected.[7] Others insist that number is much too low because many people never seek treatment. For those who do, doctors dip into an arsenal of oral drugs that can clear up three out of four fungal infections without removing the nail.[8] But don't expect miracles overnight. In about 90 percent of cases, the infection clears permanently in eight months to a year.[9]

Are Artificial Nails Safe?

Probably, but there are some hazards you should know about. First and most important is the possibility of infections. Moisture trapped under artificial nails allows bacteria and fungi to grow. In addition, false nails can cause the real nail to buckle and separate from its bed. The unprotected area is vulnerable to infection, which can result in the disfigurement or loss of the nail. Suspect an infection when the nail area gets red, itches, and hurts. You can usually blame a yellow-green, green-black, or green discoloration on a bacterium called *Pseudomonas*. A blue-green hue is often a sign of a fungal infection. To reduce the risk of infection, remove artificial nails after a few weeks.

Other possible troubles include an allergic reaction to acrylic in the nails, the glue used to attach them, or the solvent used to remove them. Nail polishes and strengtheners can provoke allergic responses, too. Watch out for infections of the cuticle. Say "No, thank you," to nail technicians who want to trim your cuticles with scissors. Make sure that the instruments used for manicures are sterilized.

Does Playing Sports or Running Track Pose Any Risks to Nails?

If you don't believe that nails are important to sports people, consider the case of pitcher Hideo Nomo of the Los Angeles Dodgers who, in 1995, bowed out of a big game with the Houston Astros after the fourth inning. The reason? A split middle fingernail was destroying his forkball, leading to three runs that cost the Dodgers the game.

Runners may not have to worry about fingernails, but toenails are of special concern. Doctors treating runners in the 1996 New York City Marathon found that more than half had experienced some kind of trauma to one or more toenails.[10] Most common were "black toenail" (bleeding beneath the nail plate) and loss of nails—both brought on by pressure and pounding inside the running shoe during long-distance training. Damage to the nail often leads to fungal infections. Nearly two in five of all 1996 New York Marathon runners reported signs of fungal infections to toenails.

The Tale of Little Red Long Nail

. . . .

White spots on nails forecast lying, anemia, wealth, a lazy temperament, health, or gifts on the way. Biting nails predicts insanity, short stature, touchy nerves, or a lifetime of thievery. People whose nails are short are tattletales. Cutting nails on Friday brings bad luck.

SUPERSTITION, FOLKLORE, AND OLD WIVES' TALES

Of all the folklore about nails, perhaps none inspires more awe and more controversy than that of the long red nail. Are tapering crimson talons refined or rude? Do they adorn beauties or bawdies? Are gleaming scarlet nails simply last year's fashion or a symbol of power—a frivolous whim for all or a rarified taste reserved for the rich and idle?

The history of coloring the nails begins in ancient Egypt—perhaps earlier. Ancient Egyptian writings on papyrus tell how Egyptian women (and often men as well) painted their eyes, rouged their cheeks, and reddened their palms and fingernails with dyes made from henna. Elaborate gold manicure tools have been found in Egyptian tombs three thousand years old.

For the Egyptians, long, red nails symbolized freedom from labor. The privilege was reserved for those of high status. Egypt's Queen Nefertiti decreed that red nail coloring could be worn only by the nobility. In China long nails carried the same message and were usually grown by men of the highest status.

Hollywood film stars of the 1930s made a new cosmetic product popular—the nitrocellulose-based nail polishes introduced after World War I. Also called nail varnish, enamel, or lacquer, nail polish first became the "in" thing among the idle rich of the French Riviera. But it was American movie idols such as Greta Garbo and Jean Harlow who made nail color and shine desirable for the masses.

Pale pinks were popular among the timid, but bright red and even black caught on with dedicated followers of fashion. Opaque shades were popular through World War II, as were frosted colors derived from the skin and scales of fish. In Paris emerald-green was the height of style. When open-toed sandals became popular, so did painting the toenails.

In the 1940s women from Maine to Monterey pined for long, polished nails like Rita Hayworth's. With the emerging chemistry of bright lipsticks and nail varnishes came the idea of glamour. The number of available colors skyrocketed, as did the popularity of long, perfectly manicured nails that could only be maintained by those who did not have to work with their hands.

By the 1960s yellow, green, blue, and purple nail polish was available to complement the black eye liner and white lipstick so popular at the time.

False nails became popular, too, for those who had neither the time nor the money to maintain a professional-quality manicure. Preformed plastic shapes were glued to the nails, then shaped and polished like the real thing. Another approach was to paint an extension of the natural nail into a form using a mixture of resin, gel, plasticizer, fibers, and solvents. Although doctors warned of allergic reactions, damage to natural nail, and infection, the fakes proved popular.

By the 1980s cosmetic companies were offering gauze, silk, or paper patches attached with lacquer for the repair of broken nails. Sculptured and wrapped nails were the trend in the 1980s, while French manicures topped the charts in the 1990s. A writer for the fashion magazine *Vogue* called a high maintenance, blood-red manicure, "a breach of office-approved good taste (and)…proof positive of a reprehensible lack of industry."[11] "Nails," wrote Becky Homan in 1995 "are a gauge of, if not sophistication, then of self-pampering and self-caring—or of downright outrageousness."[12]

Although the range of colors available in polish today seems unlimited, the number of "safe" approved coloring agents is only 34, compared with some 200 in use in the 1950s.[13] Guanine and bismuth oxychloride and coated bits of mica replaced more expensive fish parts for the creation of pearly shades. Pigments with names like D&C yellow #5, D&C reds #6, #7, and #33 can now be mixed in virtually infinite variety to produce the latest fashion shades.

After World War II, cosmetics companies started devising evocative names for their nail colors. The "in" Revlon shade of 1945 was Fatal Apple. Plumb Beautiful made it big in 1949. Where's the Fire burned up the market of 1950, followed by Fire and Ice in 1952. "Since it didn't cost any more to make a dark-red polish called Berry Bon than to make plain, dark red polish, and the one could be sold for six times the price of the other, this was not a bad strategy,"[14] writes Andrew Tobias, biographer of Charles Revson, one of the founders of Revlon.

And the strategy continues to work. In the early 1990s stars Demi Moore, Courtney Love, Uma Thurman, and Elizabeth Hurley helped make popular a Chanel shade called Vamp.

What color is Vamp? You guessed it. Dark red.

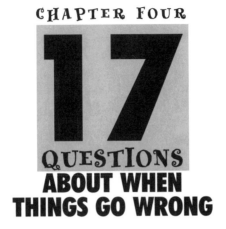

QUESTIONS ABOUT WHEN THINGS GO WRONG

Years ago, I read about a boy who had to live in a bubble...because of the weakness of his immune system and his susceptibility to disease. We are all that boy. The bubble is our skin.

• DIANE ACKERMAN •

What Happens After the Skin is Cut, Torn, or Burned?

A superficial wound affecting only the epidermis won't bleed and will heal without a scar. If the injury penetrates into the dermis, the first step in healing is the leakage of blood from damaged vessels. The blood contains the materials necessary to stop the bleeding and form a protective clot over the wound. In a series of reactions like dominos falling in a row, the clot forms.

- First, the smallest of all the blood's cells, the platelets, break and release a substance called thromboplastin. The injured skin cells release thromboplastin, too.
- Thromboplastin and other chemicals in the blood act on a protein called prothrombin, causing it to produce thrombin.

- Thrombin changes yet another protein, fibrinogen, into threads of fibrin. The mesh of fibrin traps blood cells like fish in a net. That makes the clot.

Cells and fibers in the clot form a web that contracts and pulls the edges of the wound together. That's a scab. It protects the wound against infection and facilitates the healing of skin beneath it. (That's why you should never pick or pull a scab. It will fall off when its job is done.)

As the scab is forming, the torn edges of epidermis move together, covering the layers below. Platelets release a "cocktail" of chemicals that stimulates the wound to close, brings immune cells to the injury, promotes the growth of skin cells, and starts new blood vessels forming.

Soon to arrive at the site are cells called neutrophils. They gobble up bacteria that might infect the wound and release chemicals that signal skin cells to step up their growth rate. Unless the wound is badly infected, the neutrophils finish their job within a few days and are devoured by yet another category of blood cells, the macrophages.

A mesh of fibrin envelops the blood cells below in this sequence of pictures.

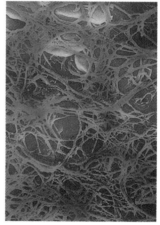

Macrophages are not just a clean-up crew. They also release chemicals that speed up cell growth and repair.

The basement layer between the dermis and epidermis acts as a framework upon which new skin is built. Epidermal cells "migrate" along the matrix below. They crawl past the edges of the cut and into the wound. Their travels are made easier by the contraction of underlying connective tissues. The shrinkage brings the edges of the wound closer together. Also, cells similar to those found in muscle form a network of interlocking fibers that pulls the wound's edges together.

Once a single layer of keratin-rich skin cells covers the wound, the movement of epidermal cells stops and the underlying layers begin to grow from the edges of the wound inward. The new tissue looks pink because numerous capillaries grow into the new skin, bringing a rich supply of nutrients and oxygen to the site.

Nerves are also important to the regrowth. Because parts of the body that have few nerve endings heal poorly, some experts think that nerve endings may release proteins that speed up the healing process.

If hair follicles survived the injury, they play a big part in healing. They grow and spread rapidly, providing many new cells to replace those that were lost. If the wound is so severe that hair follicles and sweat glands are destroyed (as they often are with serious burns), they do not grow back.

Most of the time healing is rapid and efficient, but outside factors can interfere. One study showed that women under stress took nine days longer to heal a small injury than stress-free women. The difference was greatest in the early stages of healing, when the wound was most easily infected. Blood tests showed that those under stress had less interleukin-1 beta in their blood. That's one of many proteins that the body uses to fight infection and repair damaged tissue.

What about scarring? In most cases, it's unavoidable. It results from the speeded-up production of collagen in the dermis. Too much collagen rises into the epidermis, producing the shiny, puckered mark of the scar. Collagen in undamaged skin lies in a basketweave arrangement, with fibers crossing at right angles. Collagen in a scar lies in bundles parallel to one another. As a result, scarred skin is less flexible and less elastic than uninjured skin.

Why Do Doctors Stitch Wounds?

Wounds heal, in part, because the body produces collagen to fill in the gap. The wider the gap, the more collagen produced and the bigger the scar. Sewing the wound's edges together leads to less collagen production and a smaller scar.

A large, irregular scar that grows bigger than the original wound is called a keloid. The tendency to form keloids runs in families. Dark-skinned people are more likely to form keloids than their fair-skinned friends.

What Causes Injuries to Swell?

Inflammation is the first step in the body's reaction to any injury, infection, or irritation. You know inflammation when you see it. The injured area is red, painful, swollen, and sometimes hot. Blood vessels expand in the damaged area, causing the tissue to puff up. Fluid seeps out of the stretched vessels and accumulates under the skin—that's swelling. Doctors often advise using ice for injuries because the cold reduces blood flow, thereby reducing both swelling and pain.

How Do Burns Damage the Body?

When a large area of skin is burned, the body's energy use, water balance, temperature control, and immune systems are all disrupted. Rates of fuel and oxygen use increase. The body quickly uses up all the energy reserves stored in the liver. It then begins to break down its own proteins and use them as fuel sources. Loss of fluid is a threat to the body's delicate balance of chemical processes. If severe and untreated, fluid loss can cause a sharp drop in blood pressure, called shock, which can lead to failure of the circulatory system. Imbalances in body chemistry or low levels of oxygen in the blood can trigger seizures.

What Are the Different Degrees of Burns?

Every year about two million Americans are burned or scalded seriously enough to need medical care. Some 150,000 must enter a hospital.[1] Most often, children and the elderly are the victims of accidents in the home. Burns don't just result from flames or boiling liquids. Chemicals, electric currents, and various kinds of radiation, including X rays and sunlight, can cause burns, too.

Burns are classified according to how deeply they damage the skin and how much of the body's surface is harmed. First-degree burns are relatively minor if they're not widespread. They damage only the epidermis, causing reddening and pain but no blisters or swelling. The burn usually heals within a few days, and the skin may peel, as with a sunburn.

Second-degree burns damage the skin deeper—into the dermis layer. This causes both redness and blisters. The deeper the burn, the greater the number of blisters as fluid leaks from the blood and lymph vessels that supply the dermis. Whether the healing leaves scars depends on how deep and extensive the damage was. First- and second-degree burns can often be treated at home if they are not widespread.

Third-degree burns destroy all the skin's layers, sometimes even exposing muscle and bone. Such burns are life-threatening. They must be treated by a doctor to prevent infection—the leading cause of death among burn victims. Doctors have found that pressure on healing skin lessens scarring by reducing blood supply and collagen production. That's why hospitals use slings, sleeves, stockings, and body jackets with recovering burn victims. Skin grafts are essential, and scarring is unavoidable.

What Is Skin Grafting?

Skin grafting becomes a life-or-death matter to the 13,000 people in the United States each year who suffer deep, extensive burns.[2] To graft skin, the surgeon first removes the damaged tissue from the burn, then covers the area with skin from a cadaver (dead body). This creates a temporary barrier against water loss and infection, but it can't remain in place for long. Within two or three weeks it must be taken off and replaced before the immune system rejects it. Although transfusions are needed to compensate for blood loss each time the skin is replaced, it helps the healing to begin.

In later stages the doctor removes the cadaver skin and replaces it with the patient's own skin, stripped from some other spot on the body, usually the upper body or thigh. This is called an autograft. Autografts are well accepted by the body, but the transplanted skin usually grows thinly and doesn't work as well as the original skin. Autografts fail to produce sweat and oil glands and hair follicles.

Autografts are not possible for some burn victims, who have little undamaged skin to move or are too weak to stand the operation. In such cases skin substitutes and synthetic wound coverings can save lives. One such material is Integra. It contains no cells but can act as a barrier against infection and fluid loss until an autograft becomes possible.

Certain forms of synthetic skin may someday replace cadaver skin in grafting procedures. Scientists at the Massachusetts Institute of Technology (MIT) developed a skin substitute made of collagen from calves, a complex sugar obtained from sharks, and silicone rubber. Used as a

Integra artificial skin is only 2 millimeters thick. Its collagen matrix acts as a template onto which healing skin can grow. It breaks down in about two weeks, and must be replaced with a graft.

wound cover just as cadaver skin has been, it forms a framework for the growth of the patient's own skin. When the skin substitute is removed, enough new skin has grown to form a base for skin grafts.

A slightly different form of synthetic skin uses the same synthetic material, but the patient's skin cells are "planted" in it, something like sprinkling seeds on fertile ground. The approach lets dermis and epidermis grow at the same time, eliminating the need to graft the patient's skin onto a base later on.

Someday, doctors may use artificial skin made from the lowly mussel. Researchers at the University of Delaware have found a unique combination of collagen and elastin in the mussel's bysall thread, which the animal uses to attach itself to rocks, piers, and ships. This amazing protein, five times tougher and sixteen times more flexible than the tendons that hold human muscle to bone, could be used to heal burns, seal surgical incisions, and even replace human tendons.[3] The researchers think it might even be used to make shoes and tank tracks.

Can Human Skin Be Grown in the Laboratory?

In 1975, Howard Green and James Rheinwald at Harvard Medical School first grew epidermal cells in vitro or "in glass." That means in the laboratory, in a culture, outside the living body. Today, at least two companies are providing "tissue repair" services to hospitals. Beginning with a small sample of a patient's skin, laboratory technicians can grow skin sufficient to cover as much as 45 percent of a patient's body in as little as three weeks. The skin cells are the patient's own, so the immune system does not reject them.

A Massachusetts company, Organogenesis, started with the foreskins of circumcised infant boys and grew both epidermal and dermal layers. Their product, Apligraf®, works because these cells from newborns multiply quickly. Supported on a meshlike base, a single foreskin can grow into an amazing 25,000 square meters (about 269,097 square feet) of artificial skin.[4]

Scientists are also experimenting with skin grown in the laboratory in a number of other ways. Researchers at Advanced Tissue Science (ATS) in La Jolla, California, developed Dermagraft-TC, a substitute for cadaver skin approved by the Food and Drug Administration in 1997. Dermagraft's outer layer is silicone; its inner layer, a nylon mesh.

Human skin cells grow within these layers, laying collagen, various proteins, and growth factors. Before Dermagraft is used, the cells are killed by freezing, but the structure they laid down is maintained. Like cadaver skin, it must be removed later, after healing. Another ATS product does not require removal and offers new hope to the 800,000 diabetics in the U.S. alone who suffer from chronic foot ulcers.[5] The company hopes to develop still other products for replacing cartilage in arthritic joints and repairing facial scars and deformities.

Can Doctors Perform Skin Transplants?

Transplanting skin between two people is even more difficult than transplanting a heart or a kidney. Skin cells carry on their outer surfaces a protein called human leukocyte antigen. HLA is a sort of code, and rarely do two people, other than identical twins, carry the same one. That means that the body immediately identifies a skin transplant as "not me," and sets out to destroy it. This is the problem of tissue rejection that transplant surgeons talk so much about and for which immune-depressing drugs are administered after transplant surgery.

Is There Any Way to Remove Scars?

Not completely, but there are several ways to make them less noticeable.

Z-plasty involves cutting out the scar, then pulling together small flaps of skin to cover the wound in a Z pattern. When the incision heals, it blends in with the natural creases of the face better than the scar did.

Collagen implants—injecting the body's own elastic protein into the scar—fills in pits and raises the level of a scar to blend with the skin around it. A form of collagen made from cow skin is sometimes used that way. Called Zyderm or Zyplast, it was approved by the Food and Drug Administration in the early 1980s. Another fill-in technique, the punch graft, takes a bit of skin from behind the ear and uses it to replace scar tissue.

Dermabrasion is the sanding down of the outer skin. With a rotating, high-speed wire brush or diamond wheel, a physician can scrape away the superficial layers of skin, effectively removing shallow scars like those that acne can sometimes leave. Chemical peeling achieves much the same, although it doesn't go as deep as dermabrasion. Caustic chemicals brushed over the skin cause the outer skin layers to slough off. That exposes new, living skin cells underneath and gets rid of some scars. Both techniques are risky for dark skin, which may discolor as it heals.

The newest approach to removing facial scars left by acne or chicken pox is laser resurfacing. The pulsed, carbon-dioxide laser puts out a short burst of high-intensity light so fast that the skin isn't damaged by its heat if the procedure is properly done. The light is strong enough to vaporize skin tissue to a depth about half the thickness of a human hair.[6]

How Can I Tell the Different Kinds of Rashes and Itches and Bumps Apart and Get Rid of Them?

The only way to know for sure is to see your doctor. The words that people use in casual conversation aren't much help. For example, some people call any rash eczema, but doctors restrict that term to itchy, red patches that begin in infancy and last for many years. Eczema is often associated with an allergy and may appear along with asthma, hay fever, or a runny nose.

The term dermatitis gets bantered about, too, yet it means nothing more than inflammation of the skin. To get a meaningful diagnosis, the cause of the inflammation must be determined by a professional. Doctors use the term contact dermatitis to refer to redness or inflammation of the skin that results from touching some allergen. The problem shows up only where the irritant touched the skin and appears almost immediately. Primary irritants are substances that cause damage to the skin, such as strong acids, gasoline, turpentine, paint remover, and lye. Other, milder irritants may require a longer time of exposure and affect fewer people. In this category are bubble bath, bleach, soap, and various cleaning products and cosmetics.

The rash of allergic dermatitis is caused not by the irritant itself, but by the body's response to it. An allergy is really the body's overreaction to some substance that the body can't tolerate. One out of every ten people who see a dermatologist turns out to have this kind of rash, which may not appear until days after exposure to the allergen.[7] For example, rashes as a reaction to certain drugs are common. With certain antibiotics, the rash may not develop until two weeks after the drug is taken.

The most common form of dermatitis in the United States is the red, itchy, blistered skin brought on by poison ivy or its relatives, poison oak

Beware! Poison ivy, and remember the rhyme— leaves of three, leave them be!

and poison sumac. Poisoning from these plants afflicts nearly 10 million Americans each year. A rash develops after exposure to an oil produced by these plants called urushiol. Direct contact with the plant is not necessary to start an allergic reaction. Urushiol can be carried on clothes, shoes, and even the fur of an animal. The smoke from burning poison ivy leaves can cause inflammation around the eyes. Only 10 to 15 percent of us are lucky enough to possess some natural resistance to these plants.[8]

Another commonly used term is psoriasis. This persistent condition appears as puffy red skin covered by silver-white scales that flake away quickly. It isn't an allergy, an infection, or a vitamin deficiency. Stress, infection, or arthritis can trigger psoriasis in susceptible people. Certain drugs may make it worse. It is not contagious, but it does run in families. It afflicts about 6.4 million Americans.[9]

No one knows what causes psoriasis, but we do know how it works. Normally, the process of making new skin cells takes about a month. In psoriasis, the replacement takes only three to seven days.[10] As the epidermal cells pile up—sometimes to five or ten times their normal thickness—they form puffy mounds covered with white scales of accumulated dead cells.[11] The buildup of blood vessels carrying nourishment to the rapidly dividing cells causes the redness of inflammation.

One of the most disabling skin disorders is shingles, the inflammation of a nerve. It begins with red, itchy skin and a rash of small blisters that follow the path of the nerve. A virus called varicella-zoster virus causes shingles. It's the same virus that causes chicken pox. The virus settles into the roots of nerves and lies there dormant for many years, only to travel along the nerve in later life and cause a fresh outbreak of chicken pox-like blisters on the skin. In young people, shingles is usually a mild condition that passes quickly. In older people, the pain and itching may be intense and the disease difficult to treat.

Impetigo is not so much a rash as a series of yellowish crusts often around the mouth and nose. Highly contagious, it's caused by one of several forms of the same bacteria that cause sore throats. It begins on skin damaged by a cut, bruise, or insect bite. If untreated it can spread quickly.

Prickly heat or heat rash may be caused by clogged sweat glands. The red, itchy spots have a "pins and needles" feeling, usually where sweat collects, such as the underarms or the bend of the elbow.

I Broke Out in Hives All Over Once. What Happened?

Hives are raised, blotchy, pink or red welts that pop up randomly on the surface of the skin and disappear as mysteriously as they appear, leaving no scars. Called urticaria by doctors, hives itch, sting, and burn so much that they interfere with daytime activities and block sleep at night. Hives that last longer than a day require a doctor's treatment.

As many as one in five of us will experience hives at some point in our lifetime.[12] They are probably a symptom of an allergic response in which the body releases a chemical called histamine. Histamine causes small blood vessels to widen and leak fluid.

Emotional stress can bring on hives. So can infection or drugs such as penicillin or aspirin. Pollen, animal dander, insect bites, illness, heat, or exposure to sunlight can trigger an attack. Sometimes food is the culprit. Experts estimate that food allergies may affect about one in every fourteen people.[13] Common allergens are fish, berries, nuts, cola drinks, eggs, tomatoes, citrus fruits, or milk.

Food additives may also be a problem. For example, about 15 percent of people who are allergic to aspirin are also allergic to tartrazine—also called FD&C (for "food dye and coloring") Yellow No. 5.[14] This dye is commonly added to cake mixes, candies, canned vegetables, cheese, chewing gum, hot dogs, ice cream, orange drinks, salad dressings, seasoning salts, soft drinks, and catsup.

While hives themselves are not life-threatening, anaphylactic shock is. This is an allergic response so sudden and so severe that the throat and tongue swell, impairing breathing. Blood pressure drops dangerously low. While rare, such shock is a possibility whenever a person has become sensitized to an allergen and is later exposed for a second time. Quick treatment is essential. A shot of the hormone epinephrine (also called adrenaline) causes the blood vessels to contract. That raises blood pressure and stops the flow of fluids that constricts air passages.

Why Does Lying in Bed for a Long Time Cause Sores?

Patients who are confined to a wheelchair or bed by paralysis, stroke, or coma can develop pressure ulcers, also called bedsores. If a person remains too long in one position, bony parts of the body press against the skin—for example, at the heels, ankles, elbows, or hips. The pressure impedes blood flow to the skin. The skin cells, starved of oxygen, begin to die. The dead skin breaks down and becomes vulnerable to infection. These ulcers are red, painful areas at first. Then they turn purple before the skin breaks and an open, running sore develops. Bedsores are far easier to prevent than to cure. Nurses change the position of unconscious patients every few hours. The skin is kept dry and clean. Pillows and waffle foam mattresses are used to relieve pressure and stimulate circulation.

What Are Blackheads and Whiteheads?

Both are blocked pores. Hair follicles, sebaceous (oil) glands, and sweat glands open onto the skin surface through pores. Pores cover the entire body, but those on the nose, chin, and forehead have a way of looking bigger and blacker than others. They are more obvious there because oil glands are numerous. On some parts of your face you may have as many as 2,000 oil glands in a square inch (6.45 square centimeters).[15] Oil (sebum) production sometimes widens the duct and makes it look larger.

A blackhead is a hair follicle partially plugged with dead, pigmented skin cells. Melanin, the same pigment that gives skin its color, is compacted in the plug, making it look black. The plug is porous, so oil still flows from the pore. Also called comedones (the singular is comedo), blackheads are not dirt imbedded in the skin, and no amount of washing will banish them. In fact, vigorous scrubbing may only irritate the

A blackhead (comedo) partially blocks a hair follicle.
The color comes from melanin in skin cells.

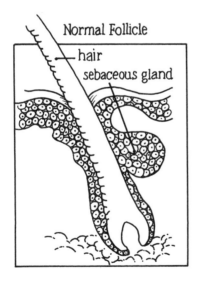
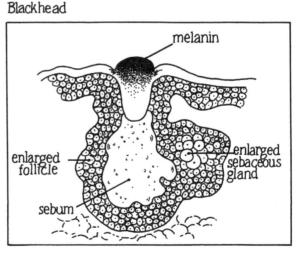

skin and speed up sebum production, making blackheads worse. Squeezing blackheads is a bad idea. It can cause permanent scarring.

Whiteheads also are plugs in the hair follicle, except that they are very small and unpigmented. Doctors sometimes call them closed comedones, because they form a nearly perfect block of the pore. The hairs in these pores are quite small, and—surprisingly—that's part of the problem. Large hairs keep pores wide open and sebum flowing freely. Small hairs let pores constrict, perhaps restricting sebum flow as well. These are the ones to watch out for. They can develop into acne.

No cosmetic product can actually shrink pores, although astringents may irritate the skin around pores causing a temporary swelling that makes pores look smaller. Hot baths and showers followed by cold packs don't shrink pores either.

What Causes Pimples and Acne?

Those innocent-looking whiteheads are the start of the problem. Sebum trapped inside the follicle makes it expand and, eventually, burst. Oil, dead cells, and bacteria can't flow out to the surface of the skin, so they invade the dermis. The body responds by making histamine and other inflammatory chemicals. Histamine makes blood vessels widen and bring more blood to the area, causing redness. Fluid seeps from the capillary walls, and the tissue swells. White blood cells of the immune system flock to the injury site, devouring bacteria and cellular debris. Dead blood and skin cells, bacteria, and oil collect beneath the skin and become the whitish ooze called pus. Doctors call these lesions papules or pustules, but you know them as pimples or zits. Get enough of them and you've got acne.

At puberty, the increased production of sex hormones stimulates the sebaceous glands to produce more oil. Sometimes the production is too great, and the skin and hair become noticeably greasy. Bacteria thrive

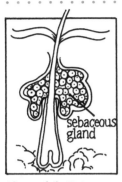
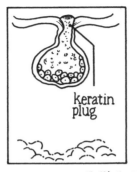
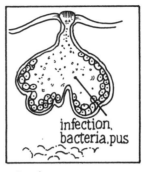

Normal Follicle Follicle breaks down Pimple

How a whitehead becomes a pimple

on the plentiful supply of sebum, and dead epidermal cells drop away from the sides of the follicle, setting the stage for the acne that affects eight of every ten teenagers.[16] Some experts think the cause may be that the immature follicles are so small, they become plugged. Acne often clears up in adulthood when pores grow bigger and sebum can flow freely, but it still shows up in one of every five adults ages 25 to 44.[17]

Many myths have made the circuit when it comes to acne. Among the innocents that have been accused of causing acne are chocolate, greasy foods, colas, allergies, and sexual thoughts or activity. Wrong on all counts. Another myth is that sunlight can cure it. "Sunbathing may temporarily improve pimples by drying them out," says dermatologist Alan Shalita, "but in the long run it seems to make acne worse."[18] The reason may be that tanning thickens the skin, increasing the possibility of clogged pores. Summer's heat can also make acne worse. Skin cells swell when the weather is humid and hot and can block the follicles. Also, oil production on the face increases 10 percent for every one-degree increase in temperature.[19]

Stress contributes to flare-ups of acne. No one knows why, but it's possible that stress triggers the production of adrenal hormones—including the male hormone, testosterone—in both women and men. Testosterone, in turn, increases the production of sebum, which can plug hair follicles and provide food for bacteria. If you skip meals, drink too much coffee, or get too little sleep, the body increases adrenaline, which helps mobilize energy reserves and keep you going. But adrenaline slows the natural shedding of the skin's horny layer. That lets dead skin cells build up and clog follicles, creating the perfect environment for acne bacteria.

Do We Really Have to Talk About Lice?

Afraid so. They're a big problem.

Lice are wingless insects about 1/8 inch (3–4 millimeters) long. They are attracted to heat, so any warm-blooded animal signals the promise of a meal to a louse. One kind, head lice, live on the human scalp and suck blood from it. The females lay whitish eggs, called "nits," on hairs close to the scalp. The nits hatch in about a week and can live for several weeks. Louse bites form itchy, red spots on the skin that look like mosquito bites. Scratching can cause secondary infections that only make the bites itch more. Head lice are easily passed from one person to another by head-to-head contact. About 6 million cases of head lice occur every year in the United States among schoolchildren.[20]

Two other kinds of lice infect human beings: pubic lice and body lice. Each is a different species, but all bite the skin and extract blood. Sexual contact, bedding, clothes, and even toilets transmit pubic lice, also called "crabs." They cause intense itching of the genital area, especially at night.

Infestations of body lice are rare in the United States. The lice bite skin but live in clothing. Destroy the clothing to get rid of body lice. Special shampoos can get rid of head and pubic lice.

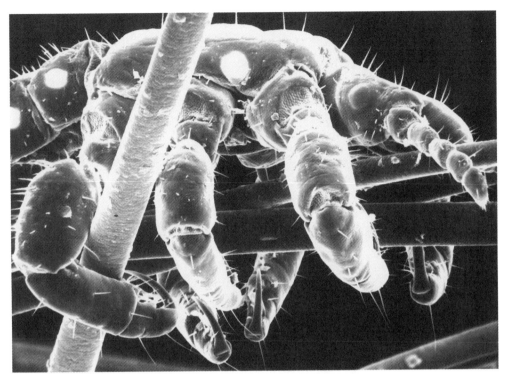

A scanning electron micrograph (SEM) of a head louse, magnified 190 times.

Another infestation, scabies, is caused not by lice but by mites so small that they can scarcely be seen without a microscope. The condition results from an allergic response to the eggs and feces that female mites deposit under the skin. Scabies is passed from one person to another by touch. The itch it brings about is tormenting, especially at night. Fortunately, doctors can prescribe an effective cure for scabies.

Still another skin eruption mistakenly blamed on "sea lice" may strike you if you swim off the coast of South Florida, Mexico, or the Caribbean. A few hours or days after the swim, red, itchy spots that look like insect bites may appear on areas of the skin that were covered by a bathing suit. Caused not by lice but by the larvae of jellyfish, which sting when trapped inside the suit, "sea-bather's itch" demands medical attention. The sting of the Portuguese man-of-war (another kind of jellyfish) may cause hives and pain. Although the sting itself is not life-threatening, swimmers stung by a jellyfish can sometimes panic and drown.

What Causes Athlete's Foot, and How Can I Get Rid of It?

Athlete's foot is a fungal infection, and you don't have to be an athlete to get it. It usually shows itself as cracked, peeling skin between the toes or as red, scaly blisters along the soles and sides of the feet. Not every skin irritation of the feet is athlete's foot. A number of other ailments can produce rashes on the feet, including allergies to shoe or dyes and skin diseases such as eczema or psoriasis. Only a doctor can diagnose athlete's foot with certainty, so it's best to seek medical advice before using over-the-counter remedies. Keeping feet dry and clean and avoiding tight shoes and socks are the best preventive measures.

What Does Frostbite Do to Skin?

Expose the skin to very cold temperatures for a long time, and the fluid between underlying skin cells freezes. Blood vessels constrict, and ice crystals form in the tissues. That's frostbite. Skin has to get much colder than the freezing point of water (0° C. or 32° F.) for frostbite to occur. Whether skin will freeze depends on the temperature, the wind-chill factor, clothing, and how long the skin is in contact with extreme cold. Exposure, poor circulation of blood (for example, if gloves or boots are too tight), and dehydration (which makes blood vessels contract thus reducing blood flow) all contribute to frostbite.

Wind or water that causes the skin to lose heat increases the chances of frostbite.

Most often affected are feet, toes, hands, fingers, nose, and ears. Mild frostbite causes the skin to redden. The skin tingles, goes numb or begins to hurt. More advanced frostbite causes skin to become waxy white or grayish yellow. The sensation of touch is lost, although there may be pain.

With prompt treatment, skin recovers if the damage is not too great. The skin thaws, becoming shiny, red, and swollen. It may sting or burn. The skin peels as it does after sunburn, but is back to normal in a few weeks. More severe frostbite can affect the deeper skin layers and even the muscle below. If left untreated, it can be serious enough to necessitate amputation of fingers or toes.

Don't cover frostbitten skin with snow, rub it, or expose it to a roaring fire. Rewarming should be slow and medical attention prompt.

Midnight Madness at Camp Sundown

. . . .

And the night shall be filled with music,
And the cares that infest the day
Shall fold their tents like Arabs,
And as silently steal away.

HENRY WADSWORTH LONGFELLOW

. . . .

Cody's skin looked fine when he was born. In fact, everything looked fine about the Lloyds' youngest son until he was more than a year old. Then Cody accompanied his parents and brothers Justin and Brandon to a joyful family picnic. All the aunts, uncles, and cousins were there.

"I suppose we were out in the sun for about 10 minutes total and most of the time Cody was in the shade of the trees," recalls his mother, Jennifer. "Anyway, that was all it took. He burnt and his skin was violent red. The burn stayed on his arms and face for about two months and then the skin started to freckle."

The Lloyds didn't realize how serious Cody's condition was until they saw a doctor. The diagnosis came as a shock: Xeroderma pigmentosum (XP for short), a rare, inherited disease that can cause freckling, burning, dryness, and flaking of the skin.[21] The skin ages prematurely, and children with XP develop skin cancers at a median age of eight, some fifty years earlier than the general population in the United States.[22] The eyes may be highly sensitive to the light and may look clouded, irritated, or bloodshot. For about one in five, deafness, blindness, physical disabilities, or learning impairments may also develop.

After Cody's XP was diagnosed, the Lloyds learned that the disorder is inherited. Each of Cody's parents carried a gene for the disease. XP showed up in Cody only because he got two XP genes—one from each parent.

At least eight different proteins are known to cause XP. The Lloyd family learned that Cody's condition is the result of a defective enzyme. When sunlight (or any other kind of ultraviolet radiation) strikes a skin cell, it can damage DNA, the master molecule in the nucleus that controls all the cell's activities. Most people make an enzyme that can repair that damage, but Cody can't. His skin cells, instead of repairing themselves, divide out of control, leading to the formation of cancerous tumors.

Operations to remove the tumors are essential—and painful in more ways than one. "Cody has had three surgeries for removing skin cancers found on his face," says his mother, "and because of that he has some scarring on his face. He is very aware of it and that makes it hard for him when he sees other children. Most of them notice it and shy away from him. That's the hardest part for me. It breaks my heart."

Cody's brothers Justin and Brandon are very protective of their little brother, because other kids who don't understand can be cruel sometimes. Jennifer and Keith Lloyd, like other parents of XP children, worry that Cody will feel isolated, alone, and different.

Caren and Dan Mahar know that fear from personal experience. Their daughter Katie was born with XP. Learning about the disorder and the problems families face, the Mahars set up the not-for-profit Xeroderma Pigmentosum Society.

More important to kids like Cody, they started Camp Sundown.

Imagine a camp where all the fun starts at 9:00 P.M. At Camp Sundown, 65 miles (105 kilometers) north of New York City, campers ride horses, eat ice cream, climb on fire trucks, and laugh with a clown— all by moonlight. The campers, all kids with XP, splash in a pool, visit petting zoos, and gobble brownies just like children everywhere—but they do it under artificial light.

Jennifer Lloyd and Cody went to Camp Sundown when Cody was five, and they can't wait to go back. "To meet children that have the same condition and see that Cody is not the only child in the world like this was a wonderful thing," Jennifer says. "Also a place where we can go and be normal staying up all night, sleeping during the day, was really something."

The Lloyds and the Mahars hope for a cure for XP. One piece of promising research concerns a substance called pTpT. This natural chemical helps skin cells repair the damage to DNA caused by UV radiation. Not only can pTpT promote skin cells to make melanin, it enhances the self-repair machinery of the skin cells. Scientists at Boston University irradiated skin cells pretreated with pTpT with damaging doses of UV light. The pTpT treated cells repaired DNA damage much faster than untreated cells. Maybe someday, a pTpT cream may help children with XP prevent skin cancers.

A campfire at Camp Sundown.

But for now, the best that parents can do is keep Cody, Katie, and the Sundown campers out of the sun whenever possible. The children must learn to wear hats and sunscreen whenever they must go outdoors. Heavy clothes are a must, because even sunshine filtered through a loosely woven garment can raise painful welts on the skin. Clouds do not block the sun's harmful rays, and even the light reflected from snow, sand, or water can be dangerous.

"Cody is six years old and pretty much an average child in every other way," says Jennifer. "I guess the only thing that makes him special is how much he knows about what kind of light he can be in. He will tell someone if they ask him about it."

Because the light from fluorescent bulbs and sunlight passing through a window can also harm kids with XP, some don't go to school. Cody learns at home with the help of a videophone link between his house and his school. A teacher's aid tutors him at home. Cody's aunts, uncles, and cousins don't gather for picnics anymore either. All their family reunions are indoors or at night.

As for that yearly writing assignment "How I Spent My Summer Vacation," perhaps Camp Sundown's oldest camper completed it best: "During the ten days that I lived at Camp Sundown, I had an absolutely fantastic, excellent, fun, and wonderful time. I forgot about my many problems, illness, and my age. At Camp Sundown I felt really human relationships, cordiality, and hospitality. I relaxed for the first time in my life. Sincerely, Ruslan Shtivel" (written July 29, 1997...in his thirtieth year.)

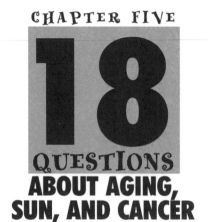

CHAPTER FIVE

18 QUESTIONS ABOUT AGING, SUN, AND CANCER

To me, fair friend, you never can be old,
For as you were when first your eye I eyed
Such seems your beauty still.

• WILLIAM SHAKESPEARE •

What Happens to Skin as People Grow Older?

While Shakespeare was happy to overlook the fading beauty of an aging loved one, most of us lack such poetic vision. Perhaps Ashley Montagu better described the mirror's tale: "As we grow older we begin to discover qualities of the skin, firmness, elasticity, texture, we had failed to notice at all until we began to lose them." Beginning in the mid-twenties, skin begins to lose the elastin fibers. The fibers start to tangle in disorganized masses as blood vessels shrivel, robbing skin of oxygen and nutrients. Aging skin also loses collagen at the rate of about one percent each year—and even faster if exposed to sunlight.[1]

Gravity, the slackening of muscles, and loss of collagen all contribute to the sagging, wrinkling skin of advancing age. After age fifty, bone mass diminishes in both men and women. The loss of both bone and fat beneath the skin lets the skin sag in the loose folds and wrinkles of old age.

As we grow older:

- a drop in hormone levels causes the epidermis to grow thin, giving that shiny parchment appearance of old age.
- the horny layer of the epidermis thickens (especially if exposed to the sun), becoming rough and scaly.
- the amount of moisture in the skin declines, so skin cracks and loses suppleness.
- the rate of manufacturing and shedding skin cells slows, and the repair of damaged cells becomes less efficient.
- sebaceous glands produce less oil, leaving skin rough and dry.
- sensitivity to drugs, chemicals, and sunlight increases.
- the number of melanocytes declines, causing hair to gray and skin to tan poorly and freckle easily.
- patches of brown, called "liver spots" or "age spots," appear often on face, neck, or hands.
- benign and malignant tumors of the skin become more likely.

Those are but a few of the changes that we see on the skin's outer surface, but below the surface—in the dermis—changes are happening, too. Blood vessels decline in number, slowing circulation and increasing sensitivity to heat and cold. Subcutaneous fat is lost, making the face, especially, look bony and hollowed. The amount of collagen decreases, and its structure changes. As a result, the skin pinches into folds more easily and is easily torn. Loss of collagen support for blood vessels means that the skin bruises more easily and wounds heal more slowly. In the face, capillaries may widen in the nose and cheeks, causing the complexion to look ruddy. Elastin fibers in the dermis thin and degenerate with age, causing wrinkles, "worry" and "laugh" lines, sagging, and rippled skin.

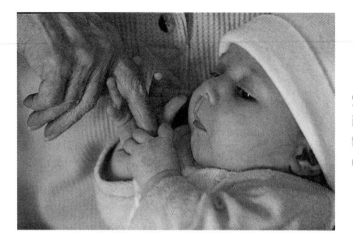

Here's the good news. Some experts believe that 80 to 90 percent of the skin changes we usually associate with aging are actually the result of the sun.[2,3] So—stay out of the sun!

Why Does Fair Skin Tan and Freckle in the Sun?

Tanning is the skin's response to damage from the sun's radiation. Making extra melanin helps protect the skin against further harm from radiation, but the shield is far from perfect.

Freckles are flat, brown spots that appear on skin exposed to the sun. The more time in the sun, the more freckles. The skin tans in round or oval spots, creating an uneven distribution of melanin. The tendency to form freckles is inherited. Freckles are more common among redheads and blonds who don't tan well than in dark-haired, dark-skinned people. Freckles fade when skin is protected from sunlight.

Why Does Sunburn Make Skin Blister and Peel?

When the skin is exposed to the sun's radiation, tiny blood vessels near the surface swell, making the skin redden. That's a natural mechanism for increasing heat loss. Too much sun causes too much swelling. Capillaries can sustain so much damage that tiny droplets of blood actually leak out of the blood vessels.

Severe burns cause blisters. The basement membrane between the dermis and epidermis holds the skin together. It can be damaged by the sun, and also by tight shoes, friction (for example, prolonged use of shovels, scissors, or other tools), infections, or disease. When the basement membrane breaks down, the two skin layers separate and serum (the liquid part of blood) leaks out of blood vessels in the dermis. The fluid accumulates just below the skin. The serum provides protection against infection. So does the skin flap over the blister. That's why you should never pull it off, even if it breaks.

Under normal conditions, you shed thousands of dead skin cells every day. You don't see or feel it happening, but your clothes, your bed, and your bathtub are littered with discarded pieces of you. Sunburn damages the epidermis and speeds up this shedding process. Damaged cells literally commit suicide. Peeling is "a mop-up operation," says Douglas Brash of Yale University.[4]

Did you know that you sunburn more quickly when you're sweating because perspiration allows the sun's rays to penetrate your skin? Perspiration can wash away your sunscreen, too. That's why you need to apply sunscreen liberally every two hours, but don't expect a lotion or cream to make it safe to stay in the sun all day. Cover up! Don't think summer is the only danger time either. Fresh snow reflects 85 percent of the sun's rays, and some 30 to 50 percent of the sun's dangerous rays pass through clouds.[5]

Maybe even more.

The villains are the ultraviolet (UV) rays that bombard the earth along with the sun's light. You can't see these rays because their wavelengths are shorter than visible light. You can't feel them either. Your skin can detect heat, cold, pain, and touch, but you have no receptors for UV radiation. The warmth you feel from the sun comes from the infrared rays, which are wavelengths longer than visible light. (Incidentally, that cozy warmth of the sun is dangerous, too. While infrared radiation alone doesn't damage skin, it augments the harmful effects of UV.)

Every time you step outdoors, you are bombarded by UV radiation of two (or maybe three) types. UVA rays (wavelength 320 to 400 nanometers) cause oxygen to combine with melanin in the skin, bringing on the tan you see immediately after exposure to the sun. UVA penetrates deep into the collagen and elastin layers of the dermis, where it weakens the skin's support structures and, over time, causes wrinkles and skin cancers. UVA rays are strongest in summer around midday.

UVB rays (wavelength 280 to 320 nanometers) are strong all day long and all year round. They penetrate less deeply into the skin than UVA, but are a thousand times more powerful.[6] While they stimulate the production of melanin and bring on a tan that takes up to a week to develop, they also damage the epidermis. Over time, such damage can lead to skin cancer. Exposure to UVB rays also causes the skin to make enzymes that destroy collagen and elastin, the proteins that make skin elastic and supple.

UVC rays (wavelength 200 to 280 nanometers) are suspected to be the most dangerous of all. That's because the shorter the wavelength, the more energy the radiation possesses. Experts disagree about whether any UVC radiation filters through the atmosphere to the earth's surface.

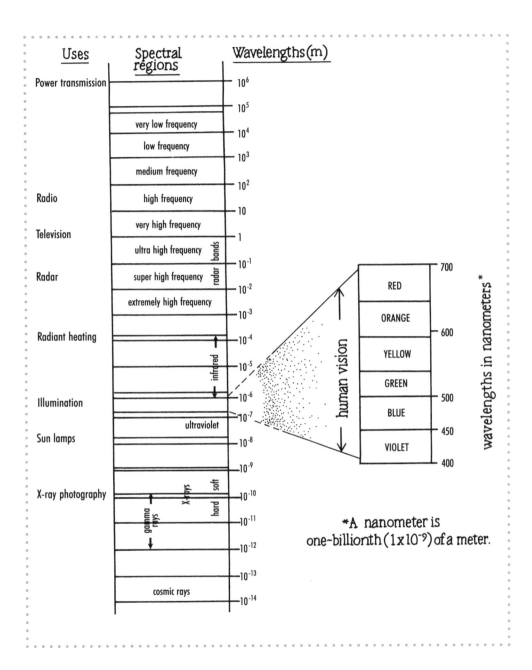

Definitely, and experts are worried.

Between 1979 and 1995, deaths from malignant melanoma (the most deadly form of skin cancer) rose in the U.S. This seems all the more worrisome because deaths from most other forms of cancer actually declined in this country after 1990.[7] Scientists think that the loss of ozone from the upper layers of the atmosphere may be at least partly to blame.

Why? Because, until recently, the layer of ozone (O_3) in the atmosphere high above the earth blocked most UVB and UVC rays. But human-made gases such as CFCs (chlorofluorocarbons) released into the air since the 1940s have reduced the amount of ozone. Now, more harmful UV rays reach the earth's surface.

Consider these statistics:

- The National Aeronautics and Space Administration estimates that the ozone layer is thinning by some 4 to 6 percent each decade.[8]
- Some 6 to 14 percent more UVB is getting through the atmosphere than it did in 1979.[9]
- Computer simulations suggest that every 1 percent decline in ozone translates into a four percent increase in the skin cancer rate.[10]

In many cities, the risk from the sun's UV rays is a routine part of the weather report. The UV index is a number from 0 to 10+ that indicates the amount of ultraviolet radiation reaching the earth's surface during the hour around noon. The greater the number, the greater the exposure to UV radiation for anyone who ventures outdoors.

The obvious way to avoid the sun's dangers is to heed the UV index and stay indoors, but nothing is ever that simple. Windows are not sufficient protection against UV. UVB rays don't get through most glass,

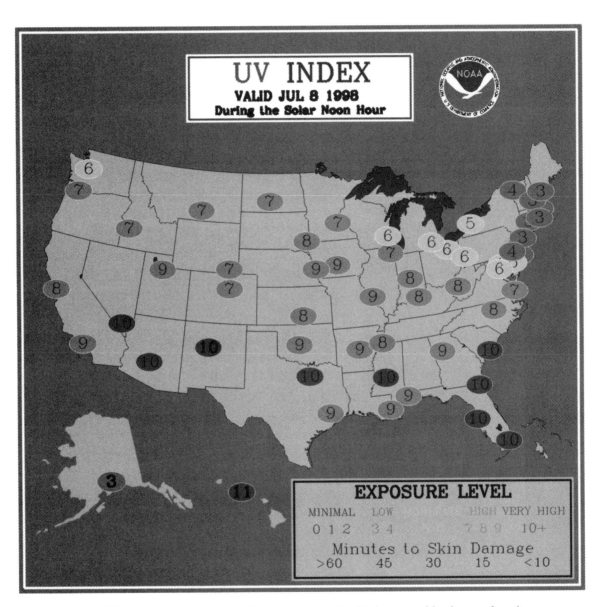

The National Weather Service estimates UV risks daily and publishes maps like this one found on the Internet.

but about 70 percent of the longer UVA rays do.[11] Both kinds are suspected as causes of wrinkles, premature aging, and skin cancer.

Will any kind of clothing help? Experts say no. If light passes through the fabric when it's held up to the sun, the clothing will let UV rays through to your skin when you wear it. Wet fabrics let more UV through than when dry. A white cotton T-shirt has an average SPF (sun protection factor) between 3 and 10, depending on its weight. Cut that in half when it gets wet.[12] A better choice is a long-sleeved shirt of a tightly woven fabric.

Cover face, hands, feet, and any other exposed skin with an SPF of 30 or higher sunscreen. Apply sunscreen generously and often, but don't expect a high SPF number to give you all-day protection. The SPF refers only to the UVB rays that are blocked. Look for preparations that also combat UVA and are labeled "broad spectrum."

How Does the Sun Cause Damage to the Skin?

When the skin is exposed to sunlight, the number of free radicals in cells increases. Free radicals are atoms or molecules that contain oxygen in a highly reactive form. They are the same kinds of compounds that cause iron to rust, stone to crumble, and paint to peel. Examples include the hydroxyl radical (OH^-) and the singlet oxygen radical (O^-).

Free radicals in large numbers can damage cells and interfere with life processes. To understand why, here's a mini-lesson in chemistry. Remember that atoms are made of a nucleus with electrons circling around it in orbits—something like planets orbiting a sun. Each orbit can hold an "ideal" number of electrons—the number that makes the atom uncharged and stable. In some orbits, the ideal number is two. If an electron is missing, the orbit has an "extra" electron, which gives the atom or molecule a negative charge.

The charged, unstable atom will steal an electron from another atom. When it does, it becomes stable itself, but turns some other atom into a free radical. This stealing of electrons can go on and on, causing damage to cell membranes, altering DNA, and interfering with life-sustaining chemical reactions.

If free radicals are so bad, you might wonder why the body tolerates them at all. Actually, they are quite useful in small numbers. They are essential to the transfer of energy from food to cells. They also combat microbes and infections.

Sunlight, smoking, pollution, drugs, and poor diet can increase the number of free radicals to dangerous levels. The body fights back, in part, with some of the nutrients that come from a healthy diet. The minerals zinc and selenium are potent antioxidants (free radical fighters) as are vitamins A, C, and E.

How effective are antioxidants in preventing skin cancers? In one study on mice, those that received large doses of vitamin A before and after exposure to cancer-causing agents remained tumor free, while those getting only small amounts developed tumors and 40 percent died. "The results provide hope that an effective treatment for malignant melanoma might be closer," said Richard Zienowicz of Brown University.[13]

Does Sunburn Affect the Immune System? Studies have found that sunburn—even a slight one—can harm the immune system, making infections of all sorts more likely. With every burn, the skin grows weaker in its ability to avoid serious damage next time.

How sunlight interferes with immune reactions is not completely understood. Part of the answer seems to involve a substance called urocanic acid. It is a natural component of the skin's outermost horny layer. When struck by the sun's rays, the urocanic acid molecule bends and twists into a distorted shape. In its altered shape, it stops the immune system from attacking skin cells damaged by the sun. That's good in a way because it gives the skin a chance to heal. But it's also bad because cancerous cells are not destroyed by the immune system. Malignant growths get a chance to start and spread.

Also, sunlight destroys a kind of white blood cell called a helper T cell. Normally, helper T cells recognize, combat, and eradicate disease-causing organisms and cancer cells. Their loss inactivates the immune response, which allows diseases and cancers to take hold.

Does Smoking Cause Wrinkles?

Study the face of a lifelong smoker and marvel at the maze of lines and blotches crinkling the leathery skin of the tobacco addict. Researchers at the University of South Florida in Tampa say that smoking interferes with the production of collagen and destroys the elastic fibers in the dermis. That lets the skin sag and crumple. Smoking also decreases the flow of blood to the skin, depriving cells of oxygen, water, and food.

The stakes are even higher than a few wrinkles. Most people know that smoking increases the risk of heart disease and lung cancer, but few know there's also a link to skin cancer. More smokers die of skin cancer than nonsmokers. "That's probably because smoking affects the immune system—the body's ability to fight off disease and cancer," says dermatologist Jeffrey Smith, who has studied the connection. "Skin cancer can do its work better in a smoker with a weakened immune system," he says.[14]

Do Anti-aging Creams and Lotions Really Work?

Some studies suggest that mixtures containing either alpha hydroxy acid or Retin-A may diminish some of the signs of aging. They work by peeling away outer, dead skin cells revealing the smoother, firmer cells beneath. Also, exposure to the sun causes the skin to make as much as 56 percent less collagen. Retin-A has shown its ability to increase collagen production.[15] Commercial preparations containing AHA probably contain too little of these chemicals to make much difference. Retin-A is available only by prescription. Both are best handled by a dermatologist or licensed plastic surgeon.

How much a person wrinkles and at what age is determined by a number of factors. Too much facial massage can rob the skin of elasticity, as can smoking, sudden weight loss, and too much scrubbing. Heredity plays a big part, as does exposure to the sun and weather.

Hormones make a difference, too. Some evidence suggests that women who take the female hormone estrogen after menopause can minimize the breakdown of collagen and maintain thicker skin as a result. Wrinkling and drying diminish in estrogen users, too. Whether the use of estrogen-containing creams slows the aging of skin is uncertain.

Although no cream has ever been proven to slow, halt, or reverse the aging process, plastic surgeons can reduce the appearance of some wrinkles. In a procedure called "wrinkle plumping," the doctor takes collagen or fat from another area of the body and injects it into the wrinkled area. Dermabrasion and chemical peeling can also reduce the appearance of wrinkles, as can the use of rapid-pulsing or scanning carbon dioxide lasers.

How Common Is
Skin Cancer?

Did you know that skin cancer:

- is the most common form of cancer in the United States?

- accounts for one of every three new cancers diagnosed each year?[16]

- is increasing faster than any other form of cancer, up 300 percent since the 1950s?[17]

- usually occurs among fair-skinned people, but anyone can get it?
- strikes men more often than women?
- is twice as likely among people who experienced even a single sunburn in childhood or adolescence?[18]

This last point raises an important question. How can skin have such a long "memory?" The harm caused by the sun is permanent because UV radiation causes "errors" in the chemical structure of DNA in the nucleus of the cell. DNA is the master molecule that carries the instruction for all cell activities. Damage it—and unless the damage is repaired—that cell and all the cells derived from it will never function normally.

Are All Skin Cancers the Same?

No. Doctors recognize three categories of skin cancers.

Four of five skin cancers are basal cell carcinomas,[19] totaling 400,000 cases in the U.S. every year.[20] These tumors grow slowly and hardly ever spread to other parts of the body. Waxy and pearl-colored, they are completely curable if removed before they have grown into deeper cell layers. The number of new cases of basal cell carcinoma has risen sharply due to the depletion of the ozone layer and the popularity of sunbathing and outdoor sports. More than 90 percent of this kind of cancer occurs on the face.[21]

Squamous cell carcinomas were found among some 100,000 people in 1996, and about 2,000 died from them.[22] This skin cancer is rarer than the basal cell type but more dangerous. Squamous cell cancers can look red and scaly, or crusty and bleeding. If left to grow, they can spread to the lymph glands and internal organs.

The third and most serious form is malignant melanoma. This kind of tumor usually begins as a black, hairless mole, but can be pale or mottled, with irregular outlines. The spreading of cancer to other locations in the body is called metastasis. Its potential for metastasis is what

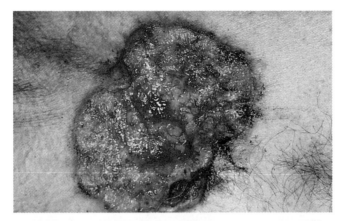

Basal cell carcinoma

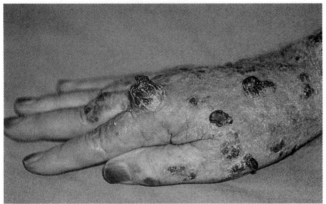

Squamous cell carcinoma

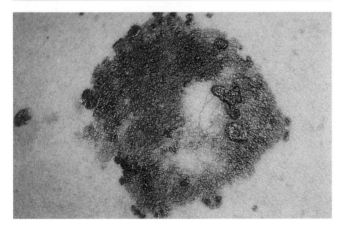

Melanoma

makes the malignant melanoma so dangerous. One in five patients diagnosed with malignant melanoma dies,[23] and the number of cases is rising rapidly—doubling every 10 to 12 years.[24] In the United States, the lifetime risk of developing melanoma is one in 84. That may not sound high, but it means that every hour, somebody in this country dies of skin cancer. That's an 1800 percent increase since 1930,[25] making melanoma the number 3 killer among all forms of cancer.[26]

In 1998 an estimated one million Americans developed skin cancer. In that same year, about 9,200 died of skin cancer, 7,300 from melanoma.[27] Yet a survey from the American Academy of Dermatology made public in 1996 showed that 42 percent of all those who were telephoned knew nothing about melanoma. Knowledge among young people, ages 18–24, was the lowest of all age groups.[28] Only 26 percent of participants could correctly identify the early signs of melanoma. More than a third didn't know that a severe sunburn increases the risk of melanoma.[29]

If caught and removed early, the cure rate for skin cancer is 95 percent. Even more encouraging is the potential for people to help themselves. Research has shown that people who take the time to examine their skin regularly—looking for changes in the size, color, or shape of moles—are as much as 63 percent less likely to die of melanoma than those who never bother.[30]

How Does Skin Cancer Spread?

The clear fluid that surrounds and nourishes all the body's cells and tissues is called lymph. Lymph moves through the body, cleaning up bacteria, viruses, waste products, and excess fluid. In its course, it follows pathways called lymph vessels that drain into lymph nodes. These nodes are soft, egg-shaped bodies about the size of a kidney bean. Nodes occur throughout the body, but are largest in the neck, underarm, and groin. Lymph nodes empty into the bloodstream. The cells of malignant melanoma can grow down through the dermis, penetrate the lymph vessels, and travel along with the lymph fluid to the lymph nodes. The cells can multiply and perhaps grow a tumor there.

Melanoma cancer cells can also spread through the bloodstream. As the skin tumor grows deep into the skin, new blood vessels develop and feed it. Some cells from the skin tumor can break off and enter a blood vessel. They can then travel through the blood, attaching themselves to the walls of blood vessels and penetrating into other organs, where they begin to grow a new tumor. Common areas for the spread of melanoma are the lungs, liver, brain, and bone. Doctors can tell by examining cancer cells under a microscope whether they came originally from a melanoma.

Are Dark-skinned People Safe From Skin Cancer?

The incidence of skin cancer is low among dark-skinned people, but no one is completely safe. Dark skin makes a lot of melanin, which helps protect from the sun's damaging rays, but the protection is not perfect. Dark skin loses its elasticity and ages in the sun just as fair skin does. Also, the tendency toward skin cancer is inherited in about 40 percent of people of all colors.[31] Scientists at the University of Miami found a gene called UVB-S that makes the skin especially sensitive to UVB radiation regardless of color. The immune systems of people with this gene quit working after UV exposure. If you are dark-skinned you should wear sunscreen, hats, and protective clothing the same as fair-skinned people.

Are Tanning Beds Safe?

No. Neither are sunlamps.

Fashion dies hard, and some people remain convinced that they look healthier and more youthful with a tan. UV light inflames skin, causing it to swell. The swelling plumps up wrinkles and causes skin to reflect more light, which can lead to the illusion of youthfulness. But it's only an illusion. Skin inflamed at the surface is damaged beneath—damaged for life.

Whether from natural or artificial sources, no tan is a safe tan. One study in Sweden showed that people under age 30 who used tanning salons were nearly eight times more likely to develop malignant melanoma than those who resisted the temptation to get that "golden, healthy" look.[32] Cancers induced by sunlamp exposure are more severe and faster growing than those caused by the sun.

Skin cancer isn't the only threat. Devotees of the instant tan risk eye damage (cataracts and harm to the retina), macular degeneration (a loss of cells in the central field of vision), compromises of the immune and circulatory systems, and irritations and rashes resulting from the interaction of the light with soaps, perfumes, and some prescription medications.

The apparently safe solution for those who crave a tan is any one of the several brands of the "self-tanning" or "sunless" creams available in most drugstores. Such instant tanners stain the surface of the skin and are sloughed off as the skin renews itself.

Someday, synthetic melanin may be available over-the-counter at the drugstore, too. John Pawelek, a scientist at Yale University, holds the patent on a compound he calls "Melasyn." Unlike natural melanin, his invention will dissolve in water, meaning it could be incorporated into a lotion to spread on the skin, producing an instant tan. Whether Melasyn would protect against sunburn isn't known.

How Can I Tell the Difference Between a Mole and Skin Cancer? You can't, not with certainty. That's why it's wise to ask a doctor to examine moles regularly. Nevertheless self-examination is critical. You should be alert to characteristics and

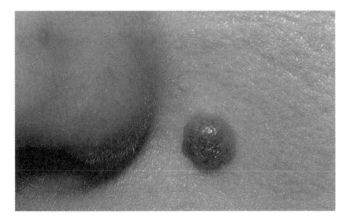

An ordinary raised mole

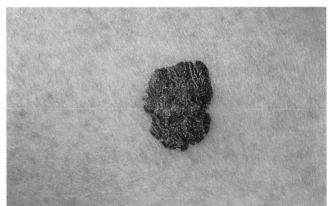

A malignant melanoma

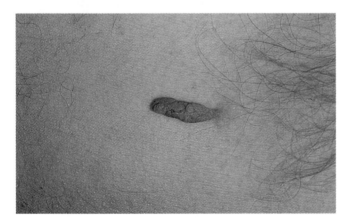

A skin tag

changes in moles that could lead to the early detection and cure of skin cancer. A simple, but effective technique for examining moles is the A-B-C-D method:

- **A** is for Asymmetry: Is one side of the mole different from the other?
- **B** is for Border: Is the edge scalloped or jagged?
- **C** is for Color: Is the color of the mole different in different areas?
- **D** is for Diameter: Is it larger than the eraser end of a pencil?

How Is Skin Cancer Treated?

Doctors diagnose skin cancer after a biopsy (removal and microscopic examination of a small piece of tissue). If the biopsy shows tumor cells, physicians have a number of treatment options to choose from:

- excision, in which the tumor and some surrounding skin are cut away and the wound is stitched closed.
- Mohs micrographic surgery, in which very thin layers of the malignant tumor are removed and checked under the microscope. This is repeated until the tissue is free of tumor. It saves the most healthy tissue and has the highest cure rate.[33]
- electrodessication, using a scraping tool and an electric needle; most widely used for removing basal cell carcinomas.
- cryosurgery, freezing with liquid nitrogen.
- radiation, often the treatment of choice when tumors recur after surgical removal or appear in sensitive, easily scarred areas such as eyelids or ears.
- carbon dioxide laser treatment, often used for basal cell carcinomas; causes little bleeding.

- topical chemotherapy, a chemical treatment that destroys squamous cell carcinomas and removes certain precancerous growths.

In the future, it may be possible to treat some skin cancers with substances that boost the body's own natural defenses. Interleukin-2 and various forms of interferon are likely candidates. Both are proteins manufactured by the immune system and proven to have cancer-fighting capacities. Another experiment is photodynamic therapy. A light-sensitizing chemical injected into the body concentrates in tumor cells. When exposed to red light from an argon-pumped laser, the cancer cells should die but healthy cells live. Another hope for the future is a vaccine to prevent skin cancers from taking hold in the first place.

How Can I Reduce My Risk of Skin Cancer?

Stay out of the sun and check your skin regularly. Most skin cancers occur in fair-haired, fair-skinned people who lack the protective pigment melanin in their skin, but anyone can get skin cancer.

Most at risk are those whose hobbies or work keep them outdoors a great deal—farmers, construction workers, athletes, and sports people. It is especially important for children and teenagers to stay out of the sun and avoid sunburn as approximately 80 percent of the sun damage to skin occurs before the age of twenty. Other risk factors include family history, certain inherited diseases, and living in a tropical climate.

Diet is a contributing factor in some 35 percent of cancer deaths in the United States.[34] Some studies suggest that an increased intake of vitamin C—found in abundance in citrus fruits, cabbage, and tomatoes—can reduce the risk of skin cancer. Eating less fat may be important, too. Researchers at Baylor College in Houston worked with 76 patients who had been treated for basal cell or squamous cell skin cancers. These people were divided into two groups. Half got no more than 20 percent of their total calories (energy) from fat. The others ate the more "typical" American diet of 36 percent fat or more.

Over a two-year period, those consuming less fat developed two-thirds fewer lesions than those eating more.[35] No one knows why a high-fat diet increases cancer rates, but it's possible that high fat intake increases the body's production of immune-regulating substances called prostaglandins. In large quantities, prostaglandins might lead to inflammation and tumor formation.

But nothing is ever simple. Martha Belury, a researcher at Purdue University, found that a chemical in fatty foods inhibits skin cancer, at least in mice. The fatty acid CLA seems to interfere with cancerous growth at all three stages of development: (1) during the initial genetic damage to cells; (2) when defective cells multiply and form tumors; and (3) when the cancer spreads to other parts of the body. CLA is found in high-fat foods—red meat, cheese, whole milk, eggs, and oil. Does that mean eat more fat, not less? No, says Belury. A low-fat diet is still a good idea, as only tiny amounts of CLA are needed.

Another way to reduce the risk of skin cancer may be to limit alcohol consumption. Researchers in Australia found that women who had had two or more drinks a day more than doubled their risk of skin cancer. Scientists at Harvard discovered that more than one drink a day increased the risk of malignant melanoma by 80 percent.[36]

The problem with such studies is that they can't prove causes, only associations. Drinking alcohol may not cause skin cancer; instead, it's possible that both alcohol use and skin cancer occur together because of some third factor not yet identified.

My Grandpa Has Keratosis. Is It Serious?

Your grandfather has one or more tumors of the skin that occur in many people in later life. To understand your grandfather's condition, you need to know which of two forms he has.

Seborrheic keratoses (the plural) are slowly-expanding growths, loosely attached to the skin of the face, chest, or back. They look pale-brown to black, waxy, and a little puffy. They can be small or large, round or oval, single or multiple. They are the result of keratin, the tough protein in the outer layer of skin, forming small plugs. They are quite common among older people. They are not infectious or contagious. Though they are never cancerous, some people have them removed for cosmetic reasons or because they itch.

Actinic keratosis is the most common of all precancerous skin conditions, affecting more than five million Americans. Most sufferers are over the age of sixty and frequently are fair-skinned.[37] It is a precancerous condition in only 5 to 10 percent of the cases.[38] Also known as solar keratosis, it is caused by exposure to the sun over many years. The dry, scaly, pink-to-brown crusts appear on the parts of the body most exposed to the sun's rays: face, ears, arms, neck, backs of the hands, and the heads of bald men. Roughly one in six people[39] develops this condition at some time, usually in later life. If treated early, the cure rate is virtually 100 percent, and cancerous lesions need never appear.

The most common treatment is cryotherapy with liquid nitrogen. Spraying or swabbing the lesions with liquid nitrogen removes them without pain or bleeding. Another procedure is scraping and controlling bleeding with an electric needle. Dermabrasion is also effective, as are chemical peels, laser surgery, and medicated creams.

To Screen or
Not to Screen?

. . . .

The tropics is no place for white-skinned men.... Invisible rays
from the upper end of the spectrum rip and tear through their
tissues, just as the X-ray ripped and tore through the tissues of so
many experimenters before they learned the danger.

JACK LONDON, *JOHN BARLEYCORN* (1913)

. . . .

Sunscreens are chemical compounds that either absorb UV rays or reflect them. The kind that absorb are more popular mostly because they are invisible. The reflective ones are also called physical blockers. They include titanium dioxide and zinc oxide, which paint the noses of skiers and lifeguards an opaque white.

Experts advise using a sunscreen with a SPF (sun protection factor) of 30 or greater. The number is a multiplier; if you would burn in 10 minutes in the sun without sunscreen, SPF 30 gives you 300 minutes or 30 times longer before burning.

Scientists at the University of Oklahoma report that proper and sustained use of a sunscreen with a protection factor of 29 reduced the incidence of precancerous lesions by 36 percent.[40] Another study concluded that using sunscreen with a protection factor of 15 during the first 18 years of life could reduce the lifetime risk of the most serious of all skin cancers by a staggering 78 percent.[41]

Dr. Marianne Berwick of the Memorial Sloan-Kettering Cancer Center in New York made headlines early in 1998 with her report that sunscreens may not protect users from developing the deadly skin cancer melanoma. "After examining the available epidemiological data and conducting our own . . . population-based study, we have found no relationship between sunscreen use at any age and the development of melanoma skin cancer," she told the American Association for the Advancement of Science.

In the United States melanoma is the most rapidly increasing form of cancer among men and the second among women (behind lung cancer), although both sexes are generally spending less total time in the sun. Engaging in outdoor activities on weekends and vacation may be to blame. Constant exposure to sun (for example, the kind farmers get) causes skin to tan and thicken, but occasional exposure increases risk because skin is vulnerable to damage.

Can sunscreen use lessen the risk for those occasionally out in the sun? Dr. Berwick found that question difficult to answer, because people often give inconsistent reports of their sunburn history and their use of sunscreen. She found that people who are sensitive to the sun engage in fewer outdoor activities and tend to wear sunscreen when they do. But

Dr. Berwick also found that, when such people develop melanoma, they do so because they are genetically susceptible to skin cancer. They will develop cancer, she says, regardless of the amount of protection from sunscreen.

Sunscreens first went on the market in 1928, but Food and Drug Administration approval was 50 years in coming. Soldiers in World War II dabbed their faces with a mixture of iron oxide and petroleum jelly. The so-called "Red Vet Pet" was thick and ugly, but it worked as a sunblock. By the 1990s sunscreens had become both invisible and conveniently packaged, and Americans were spending nearly a billion dollars for them each year.[42]

By that time, people were putting a lot of faith in sunscreens, so Dr. Berwick's challenges came as a shock. Not only are sunscreens poor prevention, Dr. Berwick claims, they may actually increase melanoma risks in susceptible individuals. If sun-sensitive people use sunscreens to let them stay out in the sun longer—thereby eliminating sunburn, which might otherwise have driven them into the shade—they expose themselves to too much sun, Berwick sunburn itself does not cause melanoma, but that it is an important sign of excessive sun exposure especially among those who are genetically susceptible because of their skin type."

Berwick's study suggested that the best predictors of melanoma risk are the number and type of moles a person has, family history, skin type, and exposure to sun in childhood as well as in the ten years prior to the development of the cancer. People who have many moles are six times more likely to develop melanoma than people who have only a few moles. Those with blond or red hair and light-colored eyes face a six-times greater risk than dark-eyed, dark-skinned people.[43]

Dr. Berwick's report prompted a barrage of objections. The American Academy of Dermatology acted immediately to counter her claims. "Overwhelming evidence supports the beneficial effects of sunscreen usage, not only in preventing painful sunburn, but also in preventing photoaging and skin cancer, including many cases of melanoma. We believe it would be irresponsible to recommend that regular use of

sunscreen be discontinued," said Roger Ceilley, president of the Academy. The Academy continues to recommend that sunscreen be used as part of an overall sun-protection regimen that includes protective clothing, staying indoors or in the shade, and staying out of the sun between ten in the morning and three in the afternoon when the sun is strongest. "To be most effective, sun protection should begin in childhood and continue throughout life," Ceilley said.[44]

Perhaps part of the problem lies in people's attitudes toward sunscreens. One in three sunbathers never bothers to apply it.[45] Others forget that a single, light application isn't enough. Sunscreens should be applied in large amounts and often. People also overestimate the effectiveness of sunscreens, says Mark Naylor of the University of Oklahoma. "Unfortunately, some individuals feel that sunscreens should provide enough protection, and they may ignore other sun safety behaviors. . . . These same individuals may ignore suspicious marks or lesions because they feel that sunscreen alone provides all the protection they need."

"Sunburn is the most preventable risk factor for skin cancer," Naylor says. "Skin type and family history cannot be changed, but all of us can take control over our sun safety habits and take precautions for protection."[46]

The most important factor in choosing a sunscreen is to select a broad-spectrum product that protects against both UVA and UVB. The SPF (sun protection factor) of the product should be at least 30 and it should be used year round, not just in summer's heat. Naylor also recommends dark clothing, a hat, and wearing a shirt while swimming.

Also, everyone should practice frequent self-examination of the skin on all parts of the body, checking for suspicious growths or changes in moles.

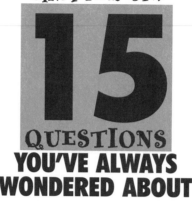

CHAPTER SIX

QUESTIONS
YOU'VE ALWAYS
WONDERED ABOUT

Tell (for you can) what it is to be wise?
'Tis but to know how little can be known.

• ALEXANDER POPE •

What Are Goose Bumps?

Chilly winds and cold weather stimulate cold receptors in the skin. These nerve endings send signals to the hypothalamus in the brain. The hypothalamus, in turn, sends a message back to the skin, causing tiny blood vessels to expand and the arrector muscles attached to hair follicles to contract. The shortening of the muscles makes the tiny, almost invisible hairs that cover most of your body stand up like–as Shakespeare described them—"quills upon the fretful porcupine." The result is the familiar appearance of "goose bumps," "goose flesh," or "goose pimples," resembling the bumpy skin of a goose plucked of its feathers.

In furry animals, this response aids in heat conservation by trapping a layer of warm air near the skin. It does the same for you, especially on parts of the body such as the forearm where visible hair grows. On less hairy parts of the body, the goose bump response probably doesn't do as much good as shivering. Step outside coatless on a blustery day and cold receptors in your skin send a message to the brain. The brain then signals muscles all over the body to contract and relax, contract and relax, again and again. The work done by the muscles generates heat and helps warm you.

Hard as you try, you can't control either goose bumps or shivering.

What Causes Stretch Marks and How Can I Get Rid of Them?

Stretch the skin too far too fast and a stretch mark is the result. Stretch marks are actually scars brought on by the breakage of the skin in its underlying layer, the dermis. The elastic fibers of the deeper layers are stretched beyond their ability to snap back. "Think of the skin as a rug and the skin's structure as the backing. Just as you can break the backing of a rug, the skin's structure can break down, too—and you get stretch marks," says expert Edward Jackson.[1]

The tendency toward stretch marks runs in families. They appear during periods of rapid growth. That may explain why many teens get stretch marks on breasts, hips, thighs, and belly during adolescence. Stretch marks of the abdomen are common in pregnancy. Weight lifters and manual laborers sometimes get stretch marks on their arms, legs, or chests. There is no cure for stretch marks, although Retin-A or pulsed dye laser treatments may fade them a little. Their red or purple color fades naturally over time.

What Are the Most Popular Forms of Plastic Surgery?

You have probably heard about facelifts and nose jobs, but some of the more common operations get considerably less publicity. For example, nearly 400,000 Americans have surgery to treat varicose veins each year.

According to the American Academy of Cosmetic Surgery, 2.6 million Americans had cosmetic surgery in 1994.[2] Although it is not surgery, the most popular procedure was the Retin-A treatment, sought by a total of nearly 900,000 men and women to improve skin texture, smooth out wrinkles, and diminish acne scars. (Because Retin-A is a strong chemical that must be handled carefully by a trained physician, the Academy classifies it along with cosmetic surgeries.)

Removal of varicose veins ranked number two at nearly 350,000, most of them women. Chemical peels, liposuction, collagen injections, and hair transplants ranked third through sixth. Among the 21 percent of cosmetic surgery patients who were male, hair transplants were the favored procedure, followed by Retin-A and liposuction.

Chemical peels produce controlled, deep, second-degree burns in order to repair acne scars, crow's feet, wrinkles of the cheeks and mouth, and blotchy color. A chemical peel can actually cause the manufacture

The most frequent cosmetic surgeries for women and men in the United States

Plastic Surgery: Women ♀

retin-A 35%
vein surgery 16%
chemical peel 10%
liposuction 10%
collagen injections 9%
all others 20%

Plastic Surgery: Men ♂

eyelid surgery 3%
nose surgery 4%
retin-A 27%
chemical peel 6%
liposuction 7%
all others 18%
hair transplants 35%

of collagen and elastin, the skin's two fundamental support proteins. The process is painful, but the improved appearance may last as long as 15 years.

Dermabrasion is the surgical removal of the surface layer of the skin by high-speed sanding. The doctor uses an abrasive wheel or wire brush rotating at high speeds to scrape away the skin. Dermabrasion is used to remove acne scars, wrinkles, tattoos, and precancerous lesions. It can diminish the puffiness of surgical scars and obliterate broken blood vessels. An alternative to dermabrasion or chemical peels is resurfacing with a carbon-dioxide laser. The laser light burns off the outer layers of skin, banishing superficial lines and pulling deeper layers tighter.

As we grow older, the skin around the eyes creases and sags, losing both its elasticity and underlying fat deposits. Weight loss, stress, and sun exposure can also make eyelids baggy. Performing an eyelid lift, the surgeon removes excess fat from the lower lid, excess skin from the upper. Results are not always satisfactory. Almost one in five people come out of this operation with too much of the white of the eye showing.[3]

Also popular are collagen injections. Collagen purified from cow skin meets a variety of cosmetic purposes. Faces that sag from age or sun exposure can be "plumped up" with a shot of collagen. The lips of some of the world's most famous cover girls have been made fuller with cow collagen. Doctors use collagen to smooth wrinkles and diminish acne scars. Collagen injections must be repeated every few months.

Another popular procedure is the tummy tuck, in which excess fat is removed from the abdomen and the abdominal muscles are stretched tighter. The traditional approach requires an incision from hip to hip, which leaves a large scar. Blood clots and inflamed veins can arise as the undesirable complications of this surgery. About 15 percent of patients who have "tummy tucks" develop bowel complications that can sometimes be serious.[4]

The alternative is liposuction in which fat-sucking tubes and surgical instruments are slipped through tiny incisions, including one around the belly button. Liposuction removes fatty tissue from the areas where fat tends to accumulate: thighs, hips, belly, and buttocks. It may also be used to reshape the face and neck. Liposuction can be done in any one of several ways. Ultrasound-assisted liposuction uses high-frequency sound waves to burst fat cells. The fat can then be vacuumed out with relatively low-volume suction devices, resulting in less bleeding, bruising, and pain than conventional methods.

About 15 of every 100 cosmetic operations is performed on a teenager. Most popular among teens are (in descending order) rhinoplasty ("nose job"), ear surgery, male breast reduction, dermabrasion, and liposuction. Breast augmentation is the procedure preferred most by those aged 19 to 34. After age 35, vein surgery ranks number one.

What Happens in a Facelift Operation?

A facelift removes excess skin and fat from the face and neck, tightens the muscles and connective tissue beneath, and redrapes the skin.

The operation begins with a shot to relax the patient and local anesthesia of the face and neck. For those who wish it, general anesthesia—"going to sleep"—may be a better option. In the traditional approach, the surgeon begins by making twin incisions on both sides of the face—following a line from the front to the back of the ear—and then makes another under the chin. In the "keyhole" approach, much smaller surgical openings are made to minimize scarring. In either case, the surgeon must free the skin of the face so that it can be lifted away from the fat and muscle underneath.

Excess fat may be removed from the neck, jaw, and cheek and used to augment thin lips and plump up lines and wrinkles, especially "mari-

Before

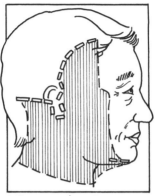

1. First incision: From above the hairline to the lower scalp.

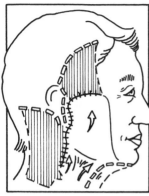

2. Tissue and muscle are separated. Fat is removed. Muscle, tightened.

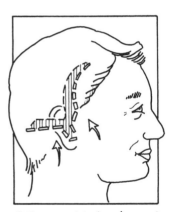

3. Excess skin is trimmed, tightened, and sewn.

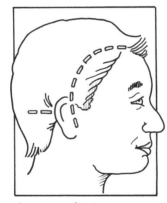

4. Scars hide in natural creases and hair.

After

The steps in a facelift

onette lines" that run vertically between the nose and mouth. Solid silicone implants are sometimes put into place to simulate higher cheekbones or a stronger jaw and chin. Loose muscles in the face and neck are tightened and the skin is sewn back together. Drains are inserted to remove excess fluid, and the face is bandaged. Bed rest helps reduce swelling, and antibiotics fight off infection. Complications are rare, but some patients experience scarring, bleeding under the skin, or damage to facial nerves resulting in loss of feeling or muscular control. Extensive bruising is the norm, so that even though the stitches can be removed in three to seven days, it may take six months or more to see the final result.[5]

In 1994, plastic surgeons performed more than 55,000 facelifts in the United States—one of every seven on a man.[6]

What Are Canker Sores?

Canker sores are small lesions that appear inside the mouth, under the lip, or beneath the tongue. At first, they have a gray-to-white center surrounded by a red area of inflammation. Later, small yellow ulcers develop, then enlarge, becoming red and painful. No one knows what causes canker sores, but they are not contagious, hereditary, or cancerous. Women get them more often than men, and the tendency to form them runs in families. Any of a large number of factors may trigger their eruption—including certain foods, drugs, fatigue, emotional stress, or illness. Nutritional deficiencies (perhaps folic acid or iron) are sometimes implicated, as are stomach upsets and diseases. Teens who wear braces sometimes get cankers from the metal rubbing against the inside of the mouth. Canker sores heal themselves without treatment, or a doctor may prescribe pain-soothing medication.

One of five Americans suffers from recurring canker sores, but as many as 4 of 5 develop fever blisters at some time in their lives.[7] These watery, red wheals appear most often on the lip or nose, but can also pop up on the chin, cheek, or inside the mouth. Also called cold sores, they are caused by a virus—most commonly Herpes simplex virus I (HSV I), which is carried by as much as 90 percent of all people around the world.[8]

The Herpes virus is a DNA virus—a protein coat surrounding a coil of DNA. DNA is the genetic material that tells cells what to do. When the viral DNA invades a normal cell, it seizes control and makes the cell start churning out copies of the virus. Because the virus "hides" inside nerve cells, it is safe from the action of antibodies of the human immune system that might otherwise destroy it. The virus lies dormant most of the time, producing sores only when provoked into action by stress, illness, fever, injury—even sunlight. When the virus makes copies of itself, the cells burst and release more viruses onto the skin to infect other cells. The watery blisters occasionally spread to other areas of the skin.

HSV spreads easily from one person to another by contact with the sores or with hands that have touched the sores. Cold sores around the lips and mouth often heal themselves in a few days and leave no scars. Doctors sometimes prescribe antiviral pills to relieve pain, heal lesions, and prevent the spread of HSV.

The same kind of virus causes genital herpes. It is the most prevalent venereal disease among young Americans today, accounting for about 15 percent of all sexually transmitted diseases in this country.[9] Close body contact through sexual activity most often transmits the infection, so condoms are an important preventive measure. Although possible, genital herpes is rarely passed from one person to another through contact with towels, drinking utensils, or toilet seats. Genital herpes outbreaks bring on pain, itching, fever, headache, and swollen lymph glands in the groin. Medical treatment is advisable.

What Is a Bruise?

A bruise is a deposit of blood under the skin. It flows from tiny capillaries that break when you bump your shin on the furniture or take the batter's pop fly in the eye. The injury starts out looking red because of hemoglobin, the red pigment in red blood cells. As blood pools under the skin, light striking the red hemoglobin bounces back and bends through many skin layers, making the bruise look blue, black, or purple. As hemoglobin breaks down over a week or two, the protein reflects more yellow-toned light and the bruise turns green, yellow, or brown.

Some people bruise more easily than others. Women get more bruises than men because their skin is thinner. The thinner the skin, the more vulnerable the capillaries to breakage. Knees and eyes are especially susceptible to bruising because they have little fat to cushion and protect them. Easy bruising may be a sign of poor blood clotting. Certain drugs ranging from aspirin to asthma drugs may interfere with blood clotting under the skin. A deficiency of vitamin C leads to easy bruising and slow healing. Vitamin C is needed to build collagen around blood vessels. With too little collagen, the capillaries suffer a lack of support and protection.

We bruise more easily as we age. Older skin is thinner skin, both in the epidermis and in the underlying collagen and elastin layers. Thin skin leaves blood vessels vulnerable to breakage at the slightest impact. Also, the skin's exposure to sunlight over the years makes it easier to damage.

What Makes People Blush?

Heat, cold, and emotions can cause the tiny capillaries of the dermis to expand. The red blood cells they carry become visible on a pale face, and a rosy complexion or blush is the result. A shock or fright can cause the opposite to occur. Capillaries contract and the fair-skinned person turns ghostly pale.

What Are Moles?

Also known as nevi (singular nevus), moles are nothing more than clumps of pigment-containing skin cells. They are pink, blue, brown, or black because they contain the pigment melanin. They can be as small as the period at the end of this sentence or big enough to cover an arm or leg. Some are flat and smooth; others are spherical and wrinkled. (See photo, page 113.)

Moles may start out flat, like freckles, then grow larger and rounder as the years pass. Some grow hairs. The average young adult has about 25 moles.[10]

Moles may also be present at birth. Many doctors recommend removal of these moles because some may develop into malignant melanoma later in life. Moles in adults are only rarely dangerous, but sudden changes in size, shape, or color may signal skin cancer, as may bleeding, itching, or pain. Perhaps 5 to 10 percent of moles become cancerous.[11]

Those to watch and have checked by a doctor

- have an irregular, asymmetric shape;
- are present from birth;
- look mixed blue and black in color;
- occur around the nails or groin.

What Is Cellulite and How Can I Get Rid of It?

Cellulite, or "orange peel skin," typically appears on the thigh and buttocks, but you may notice it also on the abdomen and upper arms. The dimply, uneven texture of the skin results from fibrous bands of connective tissue that run at right angles to the skin's surface and attach to the dermis. Fat lies between the bands, which pull on the outer skin, giving it a puckered appearance.

If you are female, you'll probably find yourself among the 88 percent of women who complain about their cellulite.[12] Women get cellulite because the female hormone, estrogen, causes the deposition of fat in thighs, hips, and buttocks. Cellulite usually appears for the first time when hormone levels are high, as during adolescence or pregnancy. Very thin or athletic women sometimes have less cellulite than their fuller-figured friends, but cellulite is not necessarily the result of being overweight.

If you have it, don't believe the advertising claims for creams and diets that promise to annihilate it. Thigh creams cannot shift the fatty deposits beneath. Massage, electric muscle-contracting machines, and heat treatments don't break down cellulite either, no matter what the claims of salons and spas. Massages and diets that promise to flush away toxins are nonsense. The body rids itself of toxins through respiration, urination, perspiration, and elimination. Herbal wraps, mud baths, and steam cabinets sweat water from tissues, making skin look temporarily smoother, but cellulite returns unscathed when the body's natural water balance is restored. Liposuction can actually make cellulite worse by taking out a layer of fat that is providing support for the skin. Losing weight doesn't help either.

The most sensible approach for people with cellulite is to keep fit, maintain a normal weight, and be proud of their normal, healthy bodies.

What Are Warts?

Warts, also called verrucas, are caused by the infection of skin cells by the human papilloma virus, or HPV. Some 40 or 50 different types of HPV are known, and 6 are associated with cancerous conditions.[13] However, malignant warts are very rare. Because a virus causes them, warts are contagious, but not from frogs and toads, as some people believe. You can pick up the wart virus in locker rooms or public showers or from family and friends. Tattoo needles can infect the skin with the wart virus.

Most warts are harmless, but some can be uncomfortable and unattractive. The typical wart is gray, rough, rounded, and painless. Flat warts are smooth, slightly raised, and skin-colored. They often appear on the face and hands. Most will vanish in time. Although as many as half go away in a year without treatment, and two-thirds clear up within two years, the American Academy of Dermatology recommends that warts be treated by a physician to prevent their spread.[14] Plantar warts are more serious. They grow inward on the soles of the feet and can make walking difficult.

Genital warts grow on the moist skin of the genital and anal regions. They pass from one person to another during sexual contact. In women they pose a small but significant risk of cervical cancer and cannot be ignored. In men they can lead to cancer of the penis, although rarely. Some 50 million Americans carry the genital form of HPV[15]—so many that virtually any sexual encounter carries the risk of infection. The body's immune system can keep HPV under control most of the time, but when genital warts appear, HPV is highly contagious.

Help from a physician is required if warts infect the genital area or become numerous, unattractive, or painful. Doctors have several different ways to remove them, including chemicals and surgery. One form of surgery uses an electric current to destroy the wart. Surgery with a carbon dioxide laser burns the wart away. Liquid nitrogen can freeze warts for removal. Acids, blistering compounds, and acid-containing corn plasters are sometimes used, too. A new and unproven technique relies on a disposable patch infused with chemicals that generate heat when exposed to oxygen. Worn over the wart for several hours daily, the patch promises removal of hand and foot warts within a month.[16] More research is needed, however.

What Causes Bags and Dark Circles Under the Eyes?

The skin under the eyes is very thin and loosely attached to the layers beneath. As the years pass, the underlying support collapses, letting the skin under the eyes fall in folds. Fat pushes into the folds and puffs out the skin. Sagging lower eyelids can also result from lack of sleep, stress, crying, or illness.

The skin below the eyes looks dark because blood vessels show through the exceptionally thin skin there. When you are tired, the flow of blood through the vessels slows, causing tiny capillaries to stretch and let their bluish color show through even more. Sinus infections and allergies can have the same effect.

What Is a Birthmark?

A birthmark is a patch of discolored skin present at, or shortly after, birth.

Vascular birthmarks result from numerous or misshapen blood vessels lying close to the skin's surface. About one in every twelve infants has a birthmark.[17] No one knows what causes them, but they don't seem to be inherited. They don't result from something the mother does during pregnancy, either, despite old wives' tales about eating strawberries or crossing paths with a black cat.

Among the hundred of different types of vascular birthmarks, three are most common:

- angel's kisses, on the forehead or eyelids; or stork bites, on the back of the neck.
- strawberry hemangiomas, bright red and slightly raised above the skin; and cavernous hemangiomas, blue.
- port-wine stains, flat reddish purple discolorations seen most often on the face, neck, arms, or legs.

Also called macular stains, angel's kisses and stork bites are small and harmless. Angel's kisses almost always disappear by the child's second birthday, but stork bites can persist into adulthood.

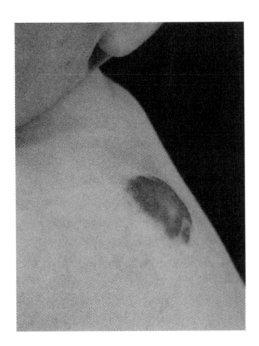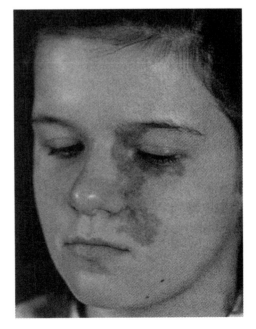

Two common birthmarks are the strawberry hemangioma, left, and the port-wine stain, right.

Hemangiomas are not usually present at birth, but appear in the first few weeks of life and grow in the first year. About one in every hundred babies has a strawberry mark.[18] Nearly three-quarters of them fade without any treatment, although they may take as long as nine or ten years to disappear completely. Doctors prefer to let them disappear naturally unless they are near the throat or the eye or in some other spot where they might interfere with normal functioning. If allowed to go away on their own, they usually leave no scar.

Port-wine stains appear on three out of every thousand babies[19] and never go away without treatment. The pulsed dye laser, which emits yellow light, is most often used to remove them. The laser emits flashes of light that last for only a few millionths of a second. The light is absorbed by the pigmented cells, leaving normal cells nearby undamaged.

Some birthmarks have nothing to do with blood vessels. They are simply accumulations of pigment in the skin. Café au lait spots are brown, flat spots which are present at birth or appear in the first few months of life. (The term is French for "coffee with milk.") Such birthmarks require attention from a doctor because they sometimes occur along with other skin diseases or even internal problems. Lasers can remove such marks and other brown colorations of skin such as the "liver spots" of old age or the freckles of the young.

"While plastic surgery cannot remove scars or birthmarks completely, new surgical techniques, combined with the use of lasers, dermabrasion, steroids and glycolic acids (chemical peels) can produce remarkable results," says Robert T. Grant, a plastic surgeon in Manhasset, New York.[20]

What Causes Fingerprints?

The way the skin grows on the tips of your fingers produces the ridges you recognize as your fingerprints. The skin all over the body is held together by millions of minute fingerlike projections called papillae. The papillae on fingers and toes line up in rows of arches, whirls, and loops.

What good are fingerprints? Ridged surfaces grip better than smooth ones. Compare a bald tire to a treaded one, and you'll get the point. The ridges are also important to the fingertips' delicate sense of touch.

It's no secret that fingerprints are a foolproof way of identifying criminals, but soon we may all be carrying "smart cards" to verify our identity. Similar to a credit card and carrying a sensor the size of a postage stamp, the card will overcome the problem of stolen automatic teller cards and forgotten secret numbers. With the card owner's fingerprint stored in the bank's computer system, one can simply touch a pad to prove that the card and the user truly belong together. "Nobody can mimic your fingerprints and you always carry your fingers around with you," says Graham Nott, a representative for Siemens, the company that is developing the card.

Other companies think that the pattern of pores in the fingertip may someday prove as useful as fingerprints for identification. Pores are the openings of sweat glands—some 10 to 20 of them on every square millimeter of fingertip. The arrangement of pores on the fingertips is as unique as a fingerprint, and computer recognition and identification from pore patterns may not be far in the future.

I Know Exercise Is Good for My Heart, But Is It Good for My Skin?

No doubt about it. In one study, researchers compared middle-aged athletes with people who didn't exercise. They found that the athletes' skin was more flexible and stronger. This may be the result of improved circulation. Exercise brings oxygen-rich blood to the living layers of the dermis, and movement promotes the manufacture of elastin.

Exercise helps you relax and improves your skin. It makes your skin and muscles feel warm and flexible and gives you that "good all over" feeling. Fluids that suffuse the skin's surface during exercise speed up the production of collagen in the dermis, says Ben Douglas of the University of Mississippi.[21] That temporarily fills in spaces around cells and makes wrinkles less noticeable.

One important tip: never wear make-up when exercising. Make-up blocks pores and interferes with sweating, the body's natural cooling mechanism.

Tattoos: Art or Agony?

. . . .

Think before you ink.

W. AXL ROSE

. . . .

Welcome to a world where flash has nothing to do with light and full-body suits aren't clothing. Sleeves don't come attached to shirts, and tat does not mean lacemaking. Collectors don't display their collections; they wear them. Scratchers are useless for an itch. Cover-ups don't. Practitioners use bars, solder, and flux but aren't metal workers. Getting ink has nothing to do with newspapers, reporters, or journalism, and the only way to practice is with a potato.

Welcome to the world of tattooing, with its long and wobbly history.

Perhaps 15,000 years ago, some cave or tree dweller noticed that soot from the fire healed inside a wound leaving a permanent mark. Experimentation with plant pigments was an obvious next step, and by the time people began writing their histories, tattooing had grown to a well-developed art form.

The ancient Egyptians practiced tattooing. Figures from the tomb of King Seti I at Karnak—dating from about 1300 B.C.—sport tattoos on both arms and legs. From Egypt, tattooing spread east. Its artistry reached high levels in Japan, southern China, and Burma, the Philip-

These three men have been tattooed with classic Japanese designs.

pines, Borneo, and the Pacific Islands. Tattooing also reached Mexico and Peru, although historians dispute how it got there.

From Egypt tattooing also spread north into Europe. The 5,300-year-old "Ice Man" found preserved in a glacier near Innsbruck, Austria, had tattooed lines on his back and a cross behind his knee. The seafaring Danes, Norsemen, and Saxons tattooed their family crests and tribal symbols on their bodies. King Harold of England who was killed in 1066 at the Battle of Hastings had "Edith" tattooed over his heart.

After the Pope banned tattooing, it virtually disappeared throughout Europe in the Middle Ages but continued to thrive elsewhere. In 1691 sailor and explorer William Dampler returned to London from the South Seas with the "Painted Prince" whose body was covered with tattoos. The prince became the darling of high society.

The prince's elaborate decorations were done in the traditional style of the Pacific Islands, the birthplace of the word "tattoo." (It comes from the Tahitian word *tatau*, meaning "to mark" or "to strike.") The name is apt. Tongans and Samoans used a wooden mallet to drive the teeth of a sharpened comb into the skin. They made black pigment from the soot of a burning candlenut mixed with fat or water. Like modern tattoos, such markings were permanent. The pigment penetrated to the second layer of skin, the dermis, which is not shed like the outer epidermis.

Historian George Burchett claims the first professional tattooist was an American. German immigrant Martin Hildebrandt set up practice in Boston and thrived during the American Civil War. Working in the thick of battle, he readily crossed the lines and tattooed both Union and Confederate soldiers.

Then, as now, tattoos have special meanings—whether social, psychological, or spiritual. For example:

• Achievement. Traditionally, sailors get bluebirds tattooed on their chests after they have sailed 5,000 sea miles (9,260 kilometers). A sailor who crossed the equator got the Roman god of the sea, Neptune, tattooed on his leg. Crossing the international dateline earned a dragon.

• War or battle. The Britons of ancient times dyed their bodies with woad, a plant belonging to the mustard family. The pigment turned them blue and allegedly terrified their enemies in battle. The Picts of ancient Scotland tattooed themselves with mammals, birds, and fish. A clan tattoo made recognizing friend and foe far easier in battle. Many clans believed also that tattoos assured continuing kinship after death.

• Celebration of an experience or event. The Crusaders often returned from the Holy Land with tattoos of crosses, St. George's battle with the dragon, Mary and Jesus, or a crowing cock.

• Membership in a group. The biker tattoos of modern times signal belonging, like the Scottish clan tattoos of centuries past. Tattoos may also signify a commonality of interest or experience. The tattooed letter M is a code for the illegal drug, marijuana. In the former Soviet Union, jailhouse tattoos followed a prescribed code: a skull for a murderer; card suits on the fingers of gamblers.

• Rank or social class. The Greeks marked spies with secret tattoos. The Romans tattooed criminals and slaves. Pacific Islanders tattooed those of the highest rank and power, such as the chief or shaman.

• Proof of adulthood or bravery. Some tribes believed that enduring the pain of tattooing assured that a woman could survive childbirth and a man could withstand injury in battle.

• Luck. Burmese men tattoo parrots on their shoulders for luck. In Thailand a tattoo of Buddha invites good fortune.

- Health or protection. The Tibetans tattoo with medicinal herbs at particular acupressure points to treat or prevent disease. In India, Hanuman, the Monkey God, can be tattooed on the shoulder to relieve the pain of a dislocation. Sailors in World War II tattooed a chicken on one foot and a pig on the other to protect against drowning.

- Animism. Some believe tattoos of dragons, tigers, eagles, and snakes give the wearer the strength and wisdom of the "totem" animal. They may also represent the animal spirit acting as guardian.

- Marriage, sexual maturity, fertility. In many cultures, tattoos signal sexual maturity. Ancient Ainu marriage rites required a woman to be properly tattooed before marriage or else face perpetual torment in the afterlife.

- Death. The Sioux Indians believed that admission to heaven required the display of tattoos. A warrior lacking them would be doomed to wander the earth forever as a ghost. Today's memorial tattoos are done in remembrance of a loved one who has died.

- Rebellion. In the 1960s some teens got tattoos for no other reason than that their parents objected.

- Beauty. The Maoris of New Zealand tattooed the lips and chin of girls to preserve their youth. In modern times tattoos decorate the bodies of old and young alike. Some say their adornments are "art for the sake of art." Some say they get them "just for the heck of it."

Whatever the reason, tattoos have boomed in popularity. In 1996 tattooing became the sixth fastest growing business in the United States—running close to such unbeatables as bagels, computers, and cellular phones. A new tattoo parlor opens every day.[22]

Acceptance is not complete, however. At least 19 states prohibit the tattooing of minors without parental consent. Tattooing is illegal in Oklahoma and South Carolina. Other states regulate and license tattoo artists. In New Hampshire tattoos may not be done at carnivals, circuses, or fairs. Some states require a doctor or nurse in attendance, and in Florida a dentist must be present. In 1997 tattooing became legal again in New York City after a thirty-year ban. The prohibition resulted from an outbreak of hepatitis B traced to unsanitary tattoo parlors.

Part of this man's full "body suit" tattoo is this traditional Samoan design.

For all its popularity, modern tattooing is only a little different from the mallet-and-comb procedures of the last century. Tattoo machines are electrically powered needle bars that can hold as many as 50 needles. The needles are dipped in colored ink. The needle bar moves up and down, piercing the skin and forcing the ink into the dermis. Hand-held tattooing machines can perform 1,500 to 3,000 insertions per minute.[23] A single needle makes fine lines. A row of needles fills in shading and heavier lines. A foot pedal controls the flow of electricity. Excess ink and oozing blood are wiped away with absorbent paper.

The first question most people ask is, "Does it hurt?" The answer seems to vary from person to person. Some people say it stings. Others grit their teeth and say they can bear it. Health risks include the possibility of infection, notably with hepatitis B or tetanus. Some people develop allergic reactions, particularly to red and yellow dyes. The pain and the risk are, perhaps, part of the mystique. "Tattoos must be worn to be tattoos, after all, and everything involved with that hard fact—the pain, the scarification, the exhibitionism, the permanence of tattooing—is what makes the phenomenon intriguing," writes Michael Kimmelman.[24]

The intrigue often wears off before the tattoo. Doctors at Skin Management Systems, Inc., estimate that half of the people who get tattoos later regret their choice and seek removal.[25] Until recently, the most common removal method was dermabrasion. The sanding away of the outer layers irritates and inflames the skin, so new skin is formed. An alternative is surgically shaving away the skin and performing a skin graft. Both methods produce less than perfect results and usually leave scars. Infection is always a risk.

Today, laser light provides a good alternative to surgery. The pulsed laser light heats the tattoo pigment, releasing it from cells so that the body can gradually clear it. Although all lasers can remove various colors of tattoos to differing degrees, the red light of the Q-switched ruby laser or alexandrite laser is especially good for erasing brown tattoos. The Q-switched neodynium-YAG laser emits two different wavelengths of light. It's best against blue-black and orange-red tattoos.

Tattoo removal with a laser can require ten or more treatments and cost more than $3,000. Results depend on the tattoo's age, location, depth, size, type, and composition of pigments—as well as the person's natural skin color. Risks of thickening, scarring, and discoloration are real, but less than with surgical techniques.

For those willing to risk a later change of heart, here's some advice. Avoid "scratchers"—untrained tattooists who operate out of market stalls, vans, or kitchens. Check for sanitary facilities and practices. Ask to see the autoclave (the steam cooker where instruments are sterilized). Make sure that needles come from sealed packages, are opened in your presence, and discarded in biomedical hazard boxes.

Professional tattooists wear latex gloves and use fresh pots of ink for each customer. They clean tables and floors with bleach or disinfectant.

Ask to see the certificate from the Alliance of Professional Tattooists certifying completion of a training course in infection control techniques.

Having second thoughts about tattooing? Consider the kind that press on with a damp cloth and wear off in a few days. Safe. Fun. Temporary.

IN CLOSING
MORE QUESTIONS THAN ANSWERS

Is the skin not a marvel of invention?
If broken, it heals itself. If torn, it repairs the rift. If
burned, it restores itself. If frozen, it rebounds anew.
In love, it radiates warmth and gladness. In offense, it
turns fiery red. And in sorrow, it becomes pallid and
ashen, a reminder of our mortality.

• MARC LAPPÉ •

What have you thought about the questions and answers on these pages? Perhaps you have been struck by how complex your skin is. It does a lot more than hold you together and make you look like you. It maintains your body temperature, protects you against disease, and keeps your water balance just right. The skin is so complicated, how can anyone possibly understand it all? The truth is, no one does. Today in laboratories all over the world, scientists are striving to unlock the secrets of human skin—secrets that could prolong life and promote health for generations in the future.

Did you notice as you read that almost every answer only raised more questions? No matter how far we have come in understanding the skin, we still have a long way to go. That deceptively simple organ that we take for granted holds more mysteries than researchers can even think about solving.

Our exploration of the workings of the human body is like exploring distant galaxies. We have a general idea of what is out there, but our knowledge is limited until we can get a closer look. With each passing year, our eyes, our instruments, and our experiments probe farther and farther past what we know into a world we can only imagine. The frontiers of space exploration are distant galaxies, pulsars, and supernovas that only giant telescopes can discern. The frontiers of medical science are molecules and atoms that can't be seen, even with today's most powerful microscopes.

Look back at the picture on page 10. The picture shows beads of perspiration on the skin. Did you figure that out, now that you have read this book? You also know, now, that your skin is a great deal more than it appears to be.

SKIN IS MORE COMPLEX THAN IT LOOKS.

One square inch (6.5 square centimeters) of skin contains...

- 19,500,000 cells
- 78 nerves
- 650 sweat glands
- 20 blood vessels
- 78 receptors for heat
- 13 receptors for cold
- 1,300 nerve endings that signal pain
- 165 nerve endings that detect touch
- 100 sebaceous glands
- 65 hairs and hair muscles
- 20 million microscopic organisms

Source: Dr. Howard Sobel, New York dermatologist.

NOTES

Chapter One

1. Alvin, Virginia, and Robert Silverstein, *Overcoming Acne: The How and Why of Healthy Skin* (New York: Morrow Junior Books, 1990), p. 8.

2. Charles Dickson, "Feeling Flaky?" (Treatments for Dandruff, Poison Ivy and Poison Sumac) *Mother Earth News* (February 12, 1996), p. 16.

3. Carol A. Turkington and Jeffrey S. Dover, *Skin Deep: An A-Z of Skin Disorders, Treatment and Health* (New York: Facts on File, 1996), p. 296. McKie says 1 in 10 in *Healthy Skin: The Facts*, p. 3.

4. Silversteins, p. 11.

5. According to Dr. Howard Sobel, New York dermatologist.

6. Silversteins, p.15.

7. Turkington and Dover, p. 176

8. Jerome Z. Litt, *Your Skin: From Acne to Zits* (New York: Dembner Books, 1989), p. 132.

9. Marc Lappé, *The Body's Edge: Our Cultural Obsession with Skin* (New York: Henry Holt, 1996), p. 43. A lower estimate of one pint (0.47 liter) appears in Reader's Digest, *The ABC's of the Human Body: A Family Answer Book,* (Pleasantville, NY: Reader's Digest Association, 1987), p. 132.

10. Rona M. McKie, *Healthy Skin: The Facts* (New York: Oxford University Press, 1992), p. 4.

11. Pioneer Productions for the Learning Channel, *Body Atlas: Skin* (New York: Ambrose Video Publishing, 1994). VHS Tape

12. *Body Atlas: Skin.*

13. Reader's Digest, p. 18.

14. Litt, *Your Skin*, p. 1.

15. Reader's Digest, *The ABC's of the Human Body* (Pleasantville, NY: Reader's Digest Association, 1987), p. 130.

16. According to Dr. Howard Sobel, New York dermatologist.

17. Litt, p. 138.

18. Joseph S. Levine and Kenneth R. Miller, *Biology: Discovering Life* (Lexington, MA: D.C. Heath, 1994), p. 226.

19. Litt, p. 141.

20. Ibid.

21. Jeffrey R. Morgan and Martin L. Yarmush, "Bioengineered Skin Substitutes," *Science & Medicine* (July/August 1997), pp. 6–9. Turkington and Dover give higher estimates, p. 295: ½ inch on the soles of the feet and 1/25 inch on the eyelids. They give the lower estimate of 1 sheet of paper for the epidermis.

22. Barney J. Kenet and Patricia Lawler, *Saving Your Skin: Prevention, Early Detection, and Treatment of Melanoma and Other Skin Cancers* (New York: Four Walls Eight Windows, 1994), p. 19.

23. Jeffrey C. May, "Dust Mite News," August, 1996, http://www.cybercom.net/~jmhi/mite.html

24. Ibid.

25. Marc McCutcheon, *The Compass in Your Nose: And Other Astonishing Facts About Humans* (New York: J.P. Tarcher, 1989), p. 117.

26. Jeffrey May, op. cit.

27. Fredric Haberman and Denise Fortino, *Your Skin: A Dermatologist's Guide to a Lifetime of Beauty and Health* (New York: Berkley Books, 1983), p. 114.

28. Jeffrey C. May, op. cit.

29. Estimates vary. See note 4. Haberman and Fortino split the difference at 1.5 pints (about 0.75 liter) per day, p. 4.

30. Lynda Jones, "Summer Survival Guide," *Science World* (May 5, 1995), p. 17.

31. Turkington and Dover, *Skin Deep*, p. 323. Haberman and Fortino give an estimated range of 2 to 5 million, p. 4.

32. Litt, p. 135.

33. At http://nevis.stir.ac.uk/~ldg/ISA/Carols1.html

34. Richard Cytowic, *The Man Who Tasted Shapes* (New York: Putnam, 1993).

35. Alison Motluk, "Two Synaesthetes Talk Colour," in *Synaesthesia: Classic and Contemporary Readings*, Simon Baron-Cohen and John E. Harrison, editors (Oxford: Blackwell, 1997), pp. 269-70.

36. Alison Motluk, "How Many People Hear in Colour?" *New Scientist* 146.1979 (May 27, 1995), p.18.

37. Judy Siegel-Itzkovich, "Listen to Those Blues and Reds," *Jerusalem Post* (January 7, 1996).

38. Alison Motluk, "Two Synaesthetes Talk Colour," pp. 269–270.

Chapter Two

1. Neil S. Sadick and Donald Charles Richardson, *Your Hair: Helping to Keep It* (Yonkers, NY: Consumer Reports Books, 1991), p. 8.

2. "Shades of Gray," *American Health* 13.6 (July/August 1994), p. 22.

3. Sadick and Richardson, p. 8.

4. Ibid., p. 10.

5. Vlado Valkovic, *Trace Elements in Human Hair* (New York: Garland STPM Press, 1977), p. 6.

6. Linda Allen Schoen and Paul Lazar, *The Look You Like: Medical Answers to 400 Questions on Skin and Hair Care* (New York: Marcel Dekker, 1990), p. 1.

7. "Raise your beauty IQ by reading these trivia tidbits on hair, makeup, exercise, skin and more!" *Teen* (November 1993), pp. 76–77.

8. Valkovic, p. 27.

9. *Teen* (November 1993), p. 77.

10. Sadick and Richardson, p.11.

11. Valkovic, p. 9

12. Schoen and Lazar, p. 5.

13. Mark McCutcheon, *The Compass in Your Nose*, p. 122.

14. Turkington and Dover, p. 147.

15. Valkovic, p. 12.

16. Schoen and Lazar, p. 11.

17. Estimates vary from six weeks (Sadick and Richardson) to three or four months (Valkovic).

18. Or about 40 yards (37 meters) a day, according to *Body Atlas: Skin* video.

19. *Teen* (November 1993), p. 77.

20. Valkovic, p. 10.

21. Marc McCutcheon, *The Compass in Your Nose*, p. 122

22. Schoen and Lazar, p. 13.

23. Doug Podolsky and Joanne Silberner, "20 Medical Stories You May Have Missed," *U.S. News & World Report* (August 3, 1992), pp. 58–60.

24. Gannett News Service, *Health and Science Briefs*, 1994.

25. Unnamed. Quoted in Podolsky and Silberner.

26. Pamela Boyer, "Say 'So Long' to White Shoulders," *Prevention*, Vol. 48 (November 1, 1996), pp. 137–140.

27. Sadick and Richardson, p. 46.

28. Schoen and Lazar, p. 15.

29. "Prevent and Cure Hair Loss," *First for Women* (October 20, 1997) p. 48.

30. Sadick and Richardson, p. 30.

31. "Developments in Laser Techniques Advance Hair Restoration." Press Release from The International Society of Hair Restoration Surgery, October 11, 1997.

32. Schoen and Lazar, p. 17.

33. Cherry Norton, "Stress Makes Working Women Lose Their Hair," *The Sunday Times* (London), November 2, 1997.

34. Thomas Maier, "Another Chance to Rub It In: FDA Approves Rogaine for Over-Counter Sales," *Newsday* (February 13, 1996), p. A06.

35. *Developments in Laser Techniques Advance Hair Restoration.*

36. Schoen and Lazar, p. 20.

37. Stephen Barrett, "Commercial Hair Analysis: Science or Scam?" *Journal of the American Medical Association* (1985), pp. 1041–1045.

38. "Hair Analysis: Is a Lock of Hair the Key to Health?" *Mayo Health Oasis*, January 30, 1997, http://www.mayo.ivi.com

39. Ibid.

40. http://www.quackwatch.com

41. Quoted in *Health* (July 1983) pp. 33–43.

Chapter Three

1. Schoen and Lazar, p. 169.

2. C.W. Fung, "Nail Diseases," *Social Hygiene Handbook*, http://www.hkma.com.hk/std/nail.htm.

3. Kathleen Doheny, "Fight This Habit Tooth and Nail," *Los Angeles Times* (October 3, 1995), Life & Style, p. 3.

4. Martin Seligman, *Learned Optimism*, (New York: Pocket Books, 1992).

5. William Nack, "The Quarterback: Near Perfection on the Field and Off, Danny Wuerffel Has Epitomized the Ideal of the College Quarterback—And in the End Showed That Nice Guys Sometimes Do Finish First," *Sports Illustrated* (January 1, 1997), pp. 24ff.

6. Pat Phillips, "New Drugs for the Nail Fungus Prevalent in Elderly," *The Journal of the American Medical Association*, July 3, 1996.

7. Kenneth R. Meisler, "Are Your Feet Ready for the Streets? Even Marathon Runners Are Slowed by Toenail Fungus," http://www.resident.com/articles/october 30/art4-10-30.html.

8. Phillips.

9. "Nail Infection: Newer Medications Tackle This Problem," *Mayo Clinic Health Letter* (May 1995; updated October 1997).

10. Kenneth R. Meisler.

11. Amy Astley, "Red-Hot Nails," *Vogue* (August 1994), p. 275.

12. Becky Homan, "Well Polished Nail Care for the '90s Giving Women the Appreciative Hand They Need," *St. Louis Post-Dispatch* (December 13, 1995), p. 4.

13. Bud Brewster, "50 Years of Cosmetic Color," *Cosmetics & Toiletries* (December 1995), pp. 107ff.

14. Quoted in Brewster.

Chapter Four

1. Geoffrey Cowley, Anne Underwood, and others, "Replacement Parts," *Newsweek* (January 27, 1997), pp. 66ff.

2. Cowley, Underwood, and others.

3. *Science*, September 19, 1997.

4. "Sowing Cells, Growing Organs," *Economist* (January 6, 1996), pp. 65–66.

5. "Advanced Tissue Sciences, Inc., and Smith & Nephew Launch Dermagraft in UK." Press release, October 8, 1997.

6. Turkington and Dover, *Skin Deep*, p. 181.

7. Litt, *Your Skin: From Acne to Zits*, p. 85.

8. Charles Dickson, "Feeling Flaky?" (Treatments for Dandruff, Poison Ivy, Poison Oak and Poison Sumac), *Mother Earth News* (February 12, 1996), p. 16.

9. The National Psoriasis Foundation.

10. Three comes from Joseph P. Bark, *Your Skin: An Owner's Guide* (Englewood Cliffs, NJ: Prentice Hall, 1995), p. 158. Turkington and Dover say seven, p. 263.

11. Arthur K. Balin, Loretta Pratt Balin, and Marietta Whittlesey, *The Life of the Skin* (New York: Bantam Books, 1997), p. 116.

12. Laura E. Skellchock, "Hives: These Wheals on the Move," *Skincare Today* (Winter/Spring 1998), p. 3.

13. Turkington and Dover, p. 129.

14. Ibid., p. 130.

15. Silversteins, *Overcoming Acne*, p. 17.

16. Sharon Snider, "Acne: Taming That Age-Old Adolescent Affliction," *FDA Consumer Magazine*, October 1990.

17. "Treating Acne Whatever Your Age," *Mayo Health Oasis*, June 16, 1997. http://www.mayo.ivi.com.

18. "It's a Myth: Sun Won't Cure Acne," *Redbook* (April 1995), p. 16.

19. *Teen* (November 1993), p. 77.

20. Turkington and Dover, p. 188.

21. So rare, in fact, that it affects only one in every 250,000 people in the U.S., according to the Xeroderma Pigmentosum Society. That's about 1,200 individuals nationwide.

22. Kenneth Kraemer, "Xeroderma Pigmentosum Knockouts," *Lancet* (February 3, 1996), p. 278.

Chapter Five

1. Balin, Balin, and Whittlesey, *The Life of the Skin*, p. 81.

2. Schoen and Lazar, p. 113. Attributed to the American Academy of Dermatology.

3. *The Body Shop Book: Skin, Hair and Body Care* (Boston: Little, Brown, 1991), p. 172.

4. Quoted in Carolyn J. Strange, "Thwarting Skin Cancer with Sun Sense," *FDA Consumer* (July/August 1995), pp. 10ff.

5. *The Body Shop Book,* p. 170.

6. Ibid.

7. Phyllis A. Wingo and others, "Cancer Incidence and Mortality, 1973–1995: A Report Card for the United States," *Cancer* (March 15, 1998).

8. Paula Kurtzwell, "Seven Steps to Safer Sunning," *FDA Consumer* (June 1996).

9. Susan Brink and Corinna Wu, "Sun Struck," *U.S. News & World Report* (June 24, 1996), p. 64.

10. Alyssa Burger, "Sun Days," *E Magazine*, Vol. 7 (July 17, 1996), p. 42.

11. "Do Windows Block the Sun's Bad Rays?" *McCall's* (July 1995), p. 12.

12. Sun Protective Clothing, http://www/bumpersfun.com.

13. "Research in Mice Indicates Potential Benefits of Vitamin A for Malignant Melanoma." Press release, American Society of Plastic & Reconstructive Surgeons, September 16, 1997.

14. "Another Gross Reason Not to Smoke," *Scholastic Choices* (October 1996), p. 4.

15. Turkington and Dover, p. 75.

16. Ibid., p. 39.

17. "Vaccine Offers Hope for Deadly Melanoma," *USA Today Magazine* (February 1996), p. 9. Turkington and Dover set the number at 500,000.

18. *The Body Shop Book*, p. 172.

19. Turkington and Dover set the figure at 83.5 percent.

20. 1996 estimates from the American Cancer Society as reported by Alyssa Burger, p. 42.

21. Turkington and Dover, p. 39.

22. Alyssa Burger, op. cit.

23. Turkington and Dover, p. 202.

24. "Vaccine Offers Hope...," *USA Today Magazine*.

25. "Screen Yourself for Melanoma: Early Diagnosis Is Crucial," *Mayo Health Oasis* (May 5, 1997), http://www.majohealth.org/mayo/9705/htm/melanoma.htm.

26. CDC, "National Melanoma/Skin Cancer Detection and Prevention Month, May 1996," *Morbidity and Mortality Weekly Report* (May 3, 1996).

27. "Use Sunscreens as Part of Sun Safety Program Says American Academy of Dermatology." Press release, American Academy of Dermatology, February 19, 1998.

28. CDC, "Survey of Knowledge of and Awareness About Melanoma—United States, 1995," *Morbidity and Mortality Weekly Report*, May 3, 1996.

29. CDC Media Advisory, May 3, 1996.

30. "Memorial Sloan Kettering: Skin Self-Exam Reduces Malignant Melanoma." Press release, January 3, 1996, http://www/newswise.com/articles/SKIN>MSK.html.

31. *The Body Shop Book*, p. 172.

32. "Deadly Tans," *American Health* (May 1995), p. 46.

33. "Skin Cancer: PDQ Information for Health Professionals," *MedNews*, National Cancer Institute, http://imsdd.med.uni-bonn.de/cancernet/101228.html.

34. "Can Cheeseburgers Fight Cancer?" *USA Today Magazine* (October 1996), p. 5.

35. "Low-fat Beats the Sun," *University of California at Berkeley Wellness Letter* (August 1995), pp. 11–12.

36. Turkington and Dover, p. 16.

37. "Blocking Skin Cancer Through Diet," *Tufts University Diet & Nutrition Letter* (July 1994), p. 8.

38. Bark, *Your Skin*, p. 182.

39. Fred Matheny, "Sun Killers," *Bicycling* (September/October 1995), pp. 58ff.

40. Aimee Lee Ball, "Lethal Sun," *Harper's Bazaar* (May 1, 1995), p. 166.

41. Alyssa Burger, p. 42.

42. Kenet and Lawler, *Saving Your Skin*, p. 170.

43. "Sunscreens May Not Protect Against Melanoma Skin Cancer." Press release, Memorial Sloan-Kettering Cancer Center, February 17, 1998.

44. "Use Sunscreens as Part of Sun Safety Program Says American Academy of Dermatology." Press release, American Academy of Dermatology, February 19, 1998.

45. Brink and Wu, "Sun Struck," p. 62.

46. "Sunscreens and Skin Cancer." Press Release, American Academy of Dermatology, March 1, 1998.

Chapter Six

1. Quoted by Hilary Stern, "What Causes Stretch Marks?" *Self* (August 1995), p. 50.

2. All Academy statistics from their Website http://www.cosmetic surgeryonline.com.

3. Doug Podolsky and Betsy Streisand, "The Price of Vanity," *U.S. News & World Report* (October 14, 1996), pp. 72–78.

4. Ibid.

5. Judy Fischer, "The End Result: A Detailed Look at Some of Today's Most Common Cosmetic Procedures," *Newsday* (November 10, 1994), p. B29.

6. Academy of Cosmetic Surgery statistics from their Website: http://www.cosmeticsurgeryonline.com

7. Figure credited to the National Institute of Dental Research, National Institutes of Health in "Fever Blisters and Canker Sores," *Consumers' Research Magazine* (June 1, 1995), p. 2.

8. Turkington and Dover, p. 74.

9. Litt, *Your Skin*, p. 63.

10. Turkington and Dover, p. 209.

11. "Benign Skin Markings: Usually Only Skin Deep, and Harmless," *Mayo Health Oasis*, http://www.mayo.ivi.com.

12. Edgar Lower, "Smoothing Over the Problem: Treatment of Cellulite," *Soap Perfumery & Cosmetics* (April 1, 1997), p. 55.

13. Schoen and Lazar, 225. The higher estimate of 50 types appears in Kathy Wollard, "How Come? Discoveries for Young People: Warts Leave in Their Own Sweet Time," *Newsday* (March 25, 1997), p. B22.

14. "Warts—Treat or Don't Treat," *Pediatrics for Parents* (January 1, 1995), p. 3.

15. Carrie Gottlieg, "The 'New' Herpes HPV Is the Most Sexually Transmitted Disease of the 90's, and Its Consequences for Women Can Be Costly," *Newsday* (January 17, 1994), p. 47. Statistics attributed to the Centers for Disease Control and Prevention, Atlanta.

16. Martin M. Stevenson, "Experimental Heat Patch Removes Warts Painlessly," *Modern Medicine* (April 1, 1996), p. 23.

17. "Benign Skin Markings: Usually Only Skin Deep, and Harmless," *Mayo Health Oasis*, http://www.mayo.ivi.com.

18. Mary Esch, "Mother Leads Crusade for Early Treatment of Strawberry Birthmarks," *Los Angeles Times* (October 6, 1997), p. A-2.

19. Phyllis Bernstein, "Not Scarred for Life," *Cosmopolitan* (September 1996), p. 180.

20. Quoted in Phyllis Bernstein, p. 180.

21. Quoted in Phil Scott, "Ahhh, Sweating to Relax," *Self* (April 1995), p. 78.

22. Mary Lord, "News You Can Use: A Hole in the Head? A Parents' Guide to Tattoos, Piercings, and Worse," *U.S. News & World Report* (November 3, 1997), p. 68.

23. "Tattoos," *New York Times Magazine* (March 17, 1996), p. 19.

24. "Tattoo Moves from Fringes to Fashion. But Is It Art?" *New York Times* (September 15, 1995), p. C1.

25. At http://www.pinkweb.com/Laser.tattoo.html

GLOSSARY

Acne: a skin condition characterized by whiteheads, pimples, and sometimes scarring caused by enlargement and inflammation of hair follicles plugged with sebum.

Actinic keratosis: rough, scaly growths on sun-damaged skin that may become cancerous.

Adrenaline: see *Epinephrine.*

Allergen: an allergy-causing substance.

Allergic dermatitis: a rash or other inflammation caused by the body's response to an allergen.

Allergy: an inflammatory reaction in cells resulting from exposure to some chemical, food, drug, metal, or other substance.

Alopecia: hair loss.

Alopecia areata: hair loss in patches.

Amino acids: the chemical building blocks of proteins.

Anagen: the growth phase of hair.

Anaphylactic shock: a sudden, severe, and life-threatening allergic response characterized by blocked breathing and plummeting blood pressure.

Athlete's foot: a fungal infection of the feet.

Apocrine glands: sweat glands localized in the armpits and groin that become active at puberty.

Arrector muscle: tiny muscles attached to hair follicles that make hair stand up.

Autograft: a skin graft transferred from one part of a patient's body to another.

Autoimmune disorder: disease in which the body's immune system attacks one's own cells as if they are foreign invaders.

Axillary hair: hair in the armpits.

Basal cells: cells in the lowest part of the epidermis that divide, producing new skin cells that migrate to the layers above.

Basal cell carcinoma: a cancer of the basal cells in the epidermis.

Birthmark: a patch of discolored skin present before, or shortly after, birth.

Blackhead: a plug of dried oil and skin cells blocking the opening of an oil gland; a comedo.

Blister: a fluid-filled swelling of the upper layers of skin.

Bruise: under the skin, a deposit of blood that has leaked from a blood vessel.

Cancer: uncontrolled abnormal cell division.

Canker sore: a sore in the mouth that is neither cancerous nor infectious.

Carcinogen: a substance or condition that causes cancer.

Catagen: the stage in the hair growth cycle in which hair is lost.

Cellulite: dimpled skin resulting from underlying deposits of fat.

Cerumen: ear wax.

Chemical peel: controlled chemical burning of the skin that prompts rebuilding of collagen, elastin, and epidermis.

Chemotherapy: treatment with anticancer drugs.

Club hair: hair that separates from the follicle and falls out during the catagen phase.

Cold sore: see *Fever blister.*

Collagen: a protein manufactured in the dermis (and other organs) that is both strong and resilient.

Comedo: see *Blackhead* and *Whitehead.*

Contact dermatitis: inflammation of the skin resulting from touching an allergy-causing substance or irritant.

Cortex: the middle of the three layers that make up the hair shaft.

Cuticle: the skin attached to the base of the fingernail. Also, the outer layer of the hair shaft.

Dandruff: scales from the scalp.

Dermabrasion: surgical removal of outer skin layers using high-speed sanding.

Dermatology: the study of skin.

Dermis: the layer of skin directly beneath the epidermis.

DNA: deoxyribonucleic acid, the fundamental molecule of heredity found in the chromosomes of the cell's nucleus. The material that makes up the gene.

Eccrine glands: sweat glands found all over the body and important to temperature regulation.

Elastin: protein manufactured in the dermis that makes skin flexible and elastic.

Electrolysis: destruction of a hair follicle by electric current.

Enzymes: proteins that catalyze (speed up) chemical reactions in living cells.

Epidermis: the outermost (surface) layer of skin.

Epinephrine: a hormone produced by the adrenal glands that stimulates the heart, contracts blood vessels, and raises blood pressure.

Estrogen: a female hormone produced by the ovaries.

Eumelanin: brown pigment of skin and hair.

Facelift: surgery to smooth wrinkles and diminish sagging of an aging face.

Fever blister: watery, red wheals caused by a Herpes simplex virus.

Fibrin: protein threads that form a blood clot.

Fibroblasts: cells of the dermis that make collagen and elastin.

First-degree burn: a burn that damages only the epidermis.

Free radical: any one of a class of charged compounds that rob other molecules of electrons and may initiate a chain reaction of damage within cells.

Frostbite: frozen skin.

Gene: a piece of DNA that controls a cell's production of a particular protein.

Goose bumps: the standing-up of hair as a result of contraction of the arrector muscles.

Hair bulb: the actively growing portion of the hair at the base of the shaft.

Hair follicle: a saclike structure in the skin from which hair grows.

Hair shaft: a strand of terminal hair composed of three layers: cuticle, cortex, and medulla.

Hives: itching, burning, nonscarring welts on the skin, usually produced by an allergic reaction.

Hormones: proteins manufactured by one organ that have an effect on another organ.

Horny layer: the skin's outermost covering of dead, hard cells. Also called the *stratum corneum.*

Hypertrichosis: overgrowth of hair.

Immune system: the integrated system of cells, tissues, and organs that protects the body against poisons and disease-causing agents.

Impetigo: an infectious skin disease caused by bacterial infection and characterized by yellow, crusty patches.

Inflammation: the body's reaction to injury or infection characterized by redness, pain, swelling, and (sometimes) increased temperature.

Interferon: a protein produced by white blood cells that has disease-fighting and cancer-fighting properties.

Interleukin: any of a class of chemicals considered important to the body's immune defenses.

Keloid: an overgrown scar.

Keratin: the protein that gives skin, nails, and hair their toughness.

Keratosis: scaly, crusty growth of skin. See *Seborrheic* and *Actinic.*

Langerhans cells: immune cells in the skin that recognize foreign invaders.

Lanugo hair: downy hair that covers a fetus.

Liposuction: surgical removal of fat with a vacuum device.

Lunula: the pale, half-moon at the base of the nail.

Lymph: the nearly colorless fluid that travels through the lymphatic circulation system and plays an important role in the body's defenses against disease.

Lymphatic system: the system of bone marrow, spleen, thymus, lymph vessels, and lymph nodes that produces, carries, and stores cells to fight infection.

Macrophages: cells that engulf neutrophils at a wound site and release chemicals that accelerate division of skin cells.

Malignant melanoma: The most deadly form of skin cancer, which begins in a melanocyte or a mole.

Matrix: the zone of the epidermis that produces a fingernail or toenail.

Medulla: the central core or pith of the hair shaft.

Melanin: the pigment produced by melanocytes that gives skin its color. Also responsible for hair color.

Melanocyte: the color-manufacturing cell in the epidermis.

Metastasis: the spread of cancer from one part of the body to another.

Mole: a colored aggregate of melanocytes on the skin surface, which may or may not grow hair.

Nail bed: the tissue beneath the nail.

Neutrophils: cells that engulf bacteria at a wound site and release chemicals that accelerate division of skin cells.

Nevus: see *Mole.*

Ozone layer: a layer in the earth's atmosphere rich in a form of oxygen (O_3) and largely responsible for filtering out ultraviolet radiation from the sun.

Papilla: a finger of connective tissue at the base of the follicle, which forms the root of the hair shaft.

Papule: see *Pimple.*

Pheomelanin: red pigment of skin and hair.

Pimple: a ruptured and inflamed hair follicle.

Platelets: the smallest of the blood cells; essential for clotting.

Port-wine stain: a flat, reddish purple birthmark.

Protein: the class of molecules responsible for much of the structure and function of living cells.

Psoriasis: an often-chronic skin disease characterized by scaly patches and skin loss.

Pubic hair: hair on the genitals.

Pustule: a pus-filled sac.

Receptors: specialized structures in the ends of nerve fibers that respond to specific stimuli (for example, heat, cold, or touch.)

Scabies: an itchy skin disease caused by a mite.

Scar: a permanent mark on the skin resulting from the regrowth of skin over an injury.

Sebaceous gland: an oil (sebum)-producing structure in the skin.

Seborrhea: dandruff.

Seborrheic dermatitis: greasy, yellowish scales on the head or chest; requires a physician's care.

Seborrheic keratosis: noncancerous areas of skin formed by plugs of keratin.

Sebum: the oily skin lubricant produced by sebaceous glands.

Second-degree burn: a burn that damages both the epidermis and the dermis.

Serum: the liquid portion of blood.

Shingles: a painful, itching skin disease caused by the localized recurrence of the chicken pox virus.

Skin graft: the surgical implantation of natural or artificial skin over a wound or burn site.

SPF: sun protection factor, a number given to a sunscreen that describes its protective capacity.

Squamous cell: one of the granular cells lying under the horny layer of the epidemis.

Squamous cell carcinoma: a type of skin cancer originating in the squamous cells of the epidermis.

Stretch marks: thin, red to silvery scars that result from stretching the skin too far.

Subcutaneous layer: the layer of collagen, connective tissue, and fat underlying the dermis.

Sunscreen: a chemical preparation applied to the skin that either reflects or absorbs the UV rays of the sun.

Sweat: perspiration; a mixture of water, salts, and waste products manufactured in the skin's sweat glands and excreted through pores in the skin.

Synesthesia: a fusion of two or more senses—for example, tasting shapes or hearing colors.

Telogen: the resting phase of the hair growth cycle.

Terminal hair: the kind of hair that grows on the head.

Testosterone: a male hormone produced by the testicles. Also present in females in small amounts (produced by the adrenal glands.)

Third-degree burn: a burn so severe that it damages the epidermis, dermis, and underlying connective tissue, muscle, or bone.

Thrombin: a substance involved in blood clotting that acts on fibrinogen to form fibrin.

Thromboplastin: a substance released by platelets; it acts on prothrombin, producing thrombin, a step in the process of forming a blood clot.

Urticaria: see *Hives.*

UV (ultraviolet) radiation: short wavelength (below the visible spectrum) radiation in any one of three types: UVA, UVB, or UVC.

UV Index: a number given as part of a weather forecast that predicts the level of ultraviolet radiation reaching a particular city on that day at solar noon.

Vaccine: a preparation that stimulates the immune system to develop means for fighting a specific disease should it strike at some later time.

Vellus hair: fine, light, nearly invisible hair that grows on most of the body.

Verruca: see *wart.*

Vitiligo: a total loss of skin color, often in patches.

Virus: a particle of DNA or RNA usually surrounded by a coat of protein that can only reproduce inside a living cell. Some viruses cause diseases in plants, animals, and even microbes.

Wart: a mildly contagious growth on the skin caused by a virus.

Whitehead: an unpigmented plug that blocks a skin pore. A closed comedo.

Xeroderma pigmentosum (XP): an inherited supersensitivity of the skin to sun that causes skin cancers and other symptoms.

FOR FURTHER INFORMATION

ARTICLES

Ball, Aimee Lee, "Lethal Sun," *Harper's Bazaar* (May 1, 1995), pp. 166–170.

Boyer, Pamela, "Say 'So Long' to White Shoulders," *Prevention* (November 1996), pp. 137ff.

Brink, Susan, and Corinna Wu, "Sun Struck," *U.S. News & World Report* (June 24, 1996), pp. 62–67.

Cowley, Geoffrey, Anne Underwood, and others, "Replacement Parts," *Newsweek* (January 27, 1997), pp. 66ff.

Delaney, Lisa, "Save Your Skin: Expert Answers to Crucial Questions About Skin Cancer," *Prevention* (April 1, 1995), pp. 76ff.

Lord, Mary, "News You Can Use: A Hole in the Head? A Parents' Guide to Tattoos, Piercings, and Worse," *U.S. News & World Report* (November 3, 1997), pp. 67–69.

Mulrine, Anna, "The Senses," *U.S. News & World Report* (January 13, 1997), pp. 50ff.

Podolsky, Doug, and Betsy Streisand, "The Price of Vanity," *U.S. News & World Report* (October 14, 1996), pp. 72–78.

Stipp, David, "Replaceable You," *Fortune* (November 25, 1996), pp. 131ff.

Strange, Carolyn J., "Second Skins," *FDA Consumer* (January 1997), pp. 12–17.

———, "Thwarting Skin Cancer with Sun Sense," *FDA Consumer* (July/August 1995), pp. 10ff.

Underwood, Anne, "The Magic of Touch," *Newsweek* (April 6, 1998), pp. 71–72.

Wickelgren, Ingrid, "Breaking the Skin Barrier," *Popular Science* (December 1996), pp. 86–90.

———, "Woman 'Hears' Colors, Man 'Tastes' Shapes," *Current Science* (January 13, 1995), pp. 4–5.

Winter, Ruth, "Do Antiaging Creams Really Work?" *Consumers Digest* (July/August 1994), pp. 61–64.

Young, Stephanie, "Moles: Beauty Marks or Trouble Spots?" *Glamour* (September 1995), pp. 84–85.

Zorpette, Glenn, "Just Scratch It," *Scientific American* (July 1995), pp. 22–23.

BOOKS AND VIDEOS

Ackerman, Diane. *A Natural History of the Senses*. New York: Random House, 1990.

Balin, Arthur K., Loretta Pratt Balin, and Marietta Whittlesey. *The Life of the Skin*. New York: Bantam Books, 1997.

Bark, Joseph P. *Your Skin: An Owner's Guide*. Englewood Cliffs, NJ: Prentice Hall, 1995.

Cytowic, Richard. *The Man Who Tasted Shapes*. New York: Putnam, 1993.

Editors of Planet Dexter. *The Hairy Book: The (Uncut) Truth About the Weirdness of Hair*. Reading, MA: Addison Wesley Longman, 1996.

Haberman, Fredric, and Denise Fortino. *Your Skin: A Dermatologist's Guide to a Lifetime of Beauty and Health*. New York: Berkley Books, 1983.

Kenet, Barney J., and Patricia Lawler. *Saving Your Skin: Prevention, Early Detection, and Treatment of Melanoma and Other Skin Cancers*. New York: Four Walls Eight Windows, 1994.

Krakow, Amy. *The Total Tattoo Book*. New York: Warner Books, 1994.

Lappé, Marc. *The Body's Edge: Our Cultural Obsession with Skin*. New York: Henry Holt, 1996.

Litt, Jerome Z. *Your Skin: From Acne to Zits*. New York: Dembner Books (Norton), 1989.

MacKie, Rona M. *Healthy Skin: The Facts*. Oxford: Oxford University Press, 1992.

Pioneer Productions for the Learning Channel. *Body Atlas: Skin*. New York: Ambrose Video Publishing, 1994. VHS Tape.

Podolsky, Doug M., and the Editors of U.S. News Books. *Skin: The Human Fabric*. Washington, DC: U.S. News Books, 1982.

Reader's Digest. *The ABC's of the Human Body*. Pleasantville, NY: Reader's Digest Association, 1987.

Schoen, Linda Allen, and Paul Lazar. *The Look You Like: Medical Answers to 400 Questions on Skin and Hair Care*. New York: Marcel Dekker, 1990.

Silverstein, Alvin, Virginia, and Robert. *Overcoming Acne: The How and Why of Healthy Skin Care*. New York: Morrow Junior Books, 1990.

Turkington, Carol A., and Jeffrey S. Dover. *Skin Deep: An A-Z of Skin Disorders, Treatments and Health*. New York: Facts on File, 1996.

ORGANIZATIONS

Alliance of Professional Tattooists
PO Box 1735
Glen Burnie, MD 21060
Trains tattooists in health and safety and educates the public.

American Academy of Cosmetic Surgery
401 North Michigan Avenue
Chicago, IL 60611
Call 1-800-A-New-You (263-9968)
Visit the Web site at http://www.cosmeticsurgeryonline.com

American Academy of Dermatology
930 North Meacham Road
Schaumburg, IL 60168
To receive a list of pamphlets, call 1-800-462-3376 or visit the Web site at http://www.aad.org

American Cancer Society
Public Information Department
1599 Clifton Road, N.E.
Atlanta, GA 30329
1-800-ACS-2345
Request pamphlets on skin cancer or download from the Web site at
http://www.cancer.org/frames.html

American Hair Loss Council
401 North Michigan Avenue
Chicago, IL 60611
Request pamphlets on alopecia and male pattern hair loss or visit the Web site
at http://www.ahlc.org/

American Society of Plastic and
    Reconstructive Surgeons
444 East Algonquin Road
Arlington Heights, IL 60005
Request the pamphlet "Plastic Surgery for Teenagers" or visit
http://www.plasticsurgery.org/

Cancer Information Service
National Cancer Institute
Information Specialist
31 Center Drive, MSC 2580
Building 31, Room 10A16
Bethesda, MD 20892
Call 1-800-4-CANCER (1-800-422-6237) to request publications from your
regional cancer information center or visit the Web site at
http://www.nci.nih.gov/hpage/cis/htm

Cosmetics, Toiletry, and Fragrance Association
1101 17th Street, NW, Suite 300
Washington, DC 20036
Ask for the pamphlet "Look Better...Feel Better" or visit the Association's Web
site at http://www.ctfa.org/

Food and Drug Administration
Office of Consumer Affairs
5600 Fishers Lane
(HFE-88)
Rockville, MD 20857
Subscribe to *FDA Consumer* or visit the Web site
http://www.fda.gov/default.htm

International Synaesthesia Association
C/O Dr. John Harrison, Academic Unit of Neuroscience
Charing Cross and Westminster Medical School
London, England
http://nevis.stir.ac.uk/~ldg/ISA/

National Alopecia Areata Foundation
710 "C" Street #11
San Rafael, CA 94901
Request the video *This Weird Thing That Makes My Hair Fall Out* or email
NAAF@compuserve.com

National Arthritis and Musculoskeletal and
    Skin Diseases Information Clearinghouse
National Institute of Arthritis and Musculoskeletal and
    Skin Diseases Information Specialist
1 AMS Circle
Bethesda, MD 20892
Request from a wide selection of pamphlets or visit the Web site at
http://www.nih.gov/niams/

National Institute of Allergy and Infectious Diseases
NIAID Office of Communications
Building 31, Room 7A-50
31 Center Drive MSC 2520
Bethesda, MD 20892
Choose from a wide selection of pamphlets and fact sheets or visit the Web site
at http://www.niaid.nih.gov/

National Pediculosis Association
P.O. Box 149
Newton, MA 02161
The sponsors of National Pediculosis Prevention Month in September.
http://www.headlice.org/

National Psoriasis Foundation
6600 SW 92nd Avenue, Suite 300
Portland, OR 97223
Read the *NPF Bulletin* or visit the Web site at http://www.psoriasis.org/

National Tattoo Association
465 Business Park Lane
Allentown, PA 18103
Publishes a newsletter and organizes conventions for tattoo artists.

National Vitiligo Foundation, Inc.
PO Box 6337
Tyler, Texas 75703
Request a fact sheet on vitiligo or visit the Web site at http://www.nvfi.org/

Skin Cancer Foundation
Public Information Director
PO Box 561
New York, NY 10156
Request the video "Skin Cancer: Preventable and Curable" or *Sun and Skin News*. Visit the Web site at
http://www.injersey.com/Living/Health/SkinCancerFound/index.htm

Xeroderma Pigmentosum Society, Inc.
PO Box 4759
Poughkeepsie, NY 12601
Request information on Xeroderma Pigmentosum or visit the Web site at http://www.xps.org/

INDEX